READ WHAT PEOPL[

D0831837

"*Guerrilla Marketing for a Bulletproof (* ... ...al training manual to successfully navigate the 21st Century career battlefield, shape it to your advantage, and attain personal and professional victory."

—Scott Durchslag, COO of Skype

"Congrats to my dear friend and devoted entrepreneur Andrew Neitlich on his new book *Guerrilla Marketing for a Bulletproof Career*. This is a brilliant career success book by a brilliant writer and educator who embodies Integrity. The same practices he preaches in his works he practices in his life. I'm honored to call him my friend and colleague."

—Leonard Marshall, NFL Hall of Fame,
two-time Superbowl Champion, Entrepreneur

"*Guerrilla Marketing for a Bulletproof Career* provides you the savvy to survey the business battlefield, armor to protect against incoming threats, tactics to manage likely encounters, and courage to lead the attack. You'll find your mindset changing from foot soldier huddled in a career foxhole avoiding the next economic bullet, to field commander moving from summit to summit. The authors do a great job speaking to you personally as time and again you find their examples reflecting your own situation and **their words calling you out toward the assertive and agile command of your own destiny**. This book is on my shortlist of must-reads for my clients."

—Gus Garcia, Garcia Group, Executive and Business Coaching,
www.execbizcoach.com

"This explosive book provides the answers to career success and fulfillment, offering clear and direct advice. It's a must read **for anyone who wants to see massive success in his or her career.**"

—Wayne Morris, CEO, Eventus Coaching,
www.eventuscoaching.co.uk

"This book is **the bible for ultimate success in your career.**"

—Helena Nyman, Success/Executive Coach, Speaker & Author,
www.ExecutiveCenterOfExcellence.com

"It's not often you can read a book that provides such practical tools, tips, and creative strategies that provide an immediate path to success. *Guerrilla Marketing for a Bulletproof Career* talks to you in a direct language with real-life examples. It helped me to immediately connect with, understand, and apply the principles. As I look to become an online marketing consultant, I now have alternatives which I need in this fast-moving technology environment. The book provides tools to further your own career with a flexible, dynamic approach that minimizes risk and **positions you for long-term security and wealth creation** in a fast-moving, uncertain market."

—Tim Vandergriend, Ebusiness Consultant,
Redalto Communications, www.redalto.com

"With clients and business partners that span six continents, I can say the insights from *Guerrilla Marketing for a Bulletproof Career* are truly applicable around the globe. In a world that is continuously shrinking due to new technologies and ways of doing business, this book is **simply a must-have for anyone serious about managing their career in today's economy. Neitlich and Levinson have nailed it.**"

—Rob Ristagno, Entrepreneur and former
McKinsey & Co. Engagement Manager

"A book that **actually delivers on how to reach YOUR OWN dreams.** Not only will you now be equipped for the inevitable, but also for the unknown."

—David O'Meara, The O'Meara Process, www.omearaprocess.com

"Back in the '70s the sports industry was revolutionized by the advent of free agency. Far less noticed but even more revolutionary has been the rise of free agency in all professions. Some, like Kobe Bryant, might choose to stay with one company for their entire career, but most businesspeople and professionals now move frequently. I know of no better way to prepare for career free agency than this insightful, eloquent book by Levinson and Neitlich. It **offers specific** concepts, strategies, and tactics for creating and maximizing the lifetime value of *your* unique career path."

—Mark P. Friedman, Principal/Founder, FastGrowth Advisors, www.fastgrowth.biz

"Andrew Neitlich provides **a new set of strategies for success** in the information age. This book is filled with practical wisdom for anyone who wants to take control of their career and capitalize on the exciting opportunities out there."

—Barbra Sundquist, Business Coach and Founder, BioTemplates.com

"I so enjoyed this book. I am an executive coach and trainer living and working in Japan, and I help Japanese businesswomen make a difference on the global stage. The recent trend in Japan is that women are gradually becoming more assertive and taking risks in either changing their jobs, career paths, or starting their own businesses. My clients are those who are lacking the assertion and confidence to start but have a desire to change. This book is **a diamond** for my market and, as someone who has recently made a risky transition, I have found this material **invaluable and motivating yet practical to use.**"

—Adrienne Gilliver, President, Connect Executive Coaching

"The career game has changed. There is a new norm! *Guerrilla Marketing for a Bulletproof Career* **captures what we owe to ourselves and need to know if we are to thrive** in what Andrew Neitlich calls 'Perpetually Gut-Wrenching Times.'"

—Len Rothman, Leadership & Executive Development, Leadership @ Work, Inc.

"Once again Andrew Neitlich has dug deep into his knowledge and experience to render up a must-have resource in this manual. Whether you're a graduate, career-changing professional, business owner, or someone reentering the workforce after a hiatus, *Guerrilla Marketing for a Bulletproof Career* covers all the bases. This book revealed not one but four 'flip the switch' strategies to build my and my clients' businesses. Slip into your camouflage fatigues and be out of the book for me was 'you are the message,' and your brand and reputation are critical. **This book will be in my top ten to recommend.**"

—Gael Bevan, Master Coaches Coach and Youth Mentor, Meta Performance International, www.meta-performance.com

"A blueprint for people to **maximize their career potential and cultivate success** ... *Guerrilla Marketing for A Bulletproof Career* provides you with marketing strategies to explode your career, in a good way! This book delivers a powerful message about career savvy and gives marketing advice that's simple, powerful, and gets results! It is a must-read for any professional who aspires to get motivated, do the impossible, and experience success. This book engages you to think outside the box of traditional career strategies."

—Susan Summons, "The Motivational Doctor," www.susanspeaksandcoaches.com

"*Guerrilla Marketing for a Bulletproof Career* provides practical ideas and tools to help people navigate today's turbulent job/business environment. Employees and employers alike will find **valuable insights to strengthen their career opportunities or advance their businesses.** My enthusiasm to continue building my coaching practice was renewed and new tools to help my clients were added to my toolbox."

—Wolfgang Weber, President, Contigro Performance Solutions Ltd., www.contigro.net

"It is said that the 'best of the best' leaders and managers are exceptional at taking very complex topics and distilling them into the essence of what is most directly relevant and important. The authors have done just this, plus they offer extremely compelling cases and stories that will inspire the reader into action. I love the simple yet elegant strategies and plan outlines that, based on both authors' track-records of success, **will certainly drive the reader to become indispensable** in their chosen career paths and **ensure ongoing opportunities** ... in fact, I have just put *Guerrilla Marketing for a Bulletproof Career* on my clients' required reading list!"

—Marshall Calman, CEO, Calman Business Advisors, www.calmanbusinessadvisors.com

"With today's unprecedented joblessness and troubled economy, this book is a real gem for helping my clients make successful career transitions. As a life and executive coach, I seek to equip myself with the best resources for helping my clients move from a state of turmoil and crisis to one of success and happiness for life. Most of us derive our sense of self worth from our careers. Therefore, being a good career coach is essential for my business. Jay Levinson and Andrew Neitlich's *Guerrilla Marketing for a Bulletproof Career* is already proving to be **a lifesaver** for me and thus for my clients. Thank you, guys, for your **invaluable insight into the tricky arena of career success!**"

—Rick Osborn, www.RickOsborn.com

"A truly incredible book! Packed with tons of useful information—you have definitely given your readers their money's worth. The past eighteen months have been truly gut-wrenching for most of us. We've realized we need to keep ourselves and our careers prepared for anything and everything. Andrew's book shows you how to do that by taking you beyond the current chaos into the next realm and lets you see that there is a better way, that there is the proverbial 'light at the end of the tunnel.' *Guerrilla Marketing for a Bulletproof Career* gives you all the strategies, tactics, and resources you need to make it happen. **If this book doesn't do it for you, nothing will!**"

—Pamela Tharp, CEO/The Athena Group,
www.successfulwomancoaching.com

"A timely book that diverts your attention from the challenges of economic uncertainty to an opportunistic mindset, preparing you for greater success. **A must-read for entrepreneurs, students, employees, and anyone who wants to achieve leadership in their professional and personal lives.** Jay Levinson and Andrew Neitlich share their wealth of knowledge and expertise to prepare you for resilience and agility, pushing you to adapt to change, and arms you with a 'bulletproof vest' for a triumphant career adventure."

—Linda Le, Executive Coach, Australia

"Andrew Neitlich has done it again! He has taken an often terrifying topic like career change and transition and packaged a powerful process into **a real-time, effective, essential guide**. *Guerrilla Marketing for a Bulletproof Career* arms you with the tools required to make powerful decisions and

realize an extraordinary career. A person ready to take charge of their life will love this book."

—Kristina Mercier, CPC, CEC, CCC; Life and Career Designer,
www.kristinamercier.com

"This book is a must-read for anyone who wants to bulletproof their career or business. Andrew's simple yet powerful way of conveying practical and useful strategies backed by personal case studies make this book **the best career development tool I have read** to date. If you are serious at all about growing your career or your business, you will want to read this book over and over until you have mastered Andrew's techniques. Thanks, Andrew, for all that you have done for my business and my career."

—Rick Crain, President, Breakthrough Business Solutions, LLC

"The tools in *Guerrilla Marketing for a Bulletproof Career* are **not only career advice**, they are **the things you should do to have a meaningful life**. As always, Andrew Neitlich and Jay Conrad Levinson get to the point and explain what is important."

—Paul Ryan, Managing Partner, Hayfield Capital LLC,
www.hayfieldcapital.com

"Agility on the tennis court is the ability to stop, start, and move in any direction with explosive energy. *Guerrilla Marketing for a Bulletproof Career* shows the reader how important it is to be agile in the workforce as well as for career development to **keep you ahead of the career game and one step faster than the competition**."

—Steve Martin, Tennis Professional and Publisher, www.fitstocks.com

GUERRILLA MARKETING

FOR A BULLETPROOF CAREER

How to Attract Ongoing Opportunities in
Perpetually Gut-Wrenching Times, for Entrepreneurs,
Employees, and Everyone in Between

JAY CONRAD LEVINSON
& ANDREW NEITLICH

NEW YORK

CONTENTS

ACKNOWLEDGMENTS

JAY CONRAD LEVINSON

I owe heartfelt acknowledgement in this book to Andrew Neitlich, who did all the heavy lifting and supplied the brilliance with which this book has been written. If you benefit from his insight, give all the credit to him, for I was merely along for the ride. My main contribution has been to provide the guerrilla spirit that has infused him. He has done a wonderful job absorbing it and spreading it to everyone who reads the words he has written.

ANDREW NEITLICH

I am forever grateful to Jim Reilly, who was generous enough to introduce me to Jay Conrad Levinson. Jay has been a hero of mine for decades, and it is an honor and a highlight of my career to have this opportunity to work with him. John Lankford and Corey Crowder deserve special acknowledgement, too. Our work together creating career transition programs for elite athletes started me down the road that led to this book. Thanks are also due to the many members of The Center for Executive Coaching and The Center for Career Coaching who shared with me their own stories and ideas about creating a successful career. Nancy McAward and Pam Tharp kindly volunteered their time to make fantastic edits to the book, which I appreciate deeply. Eternal thanks go to my wife Elena, a successful entrepreneur and author who simultaneously wrote a book while I wrote this one—except she wrote hers while holding our third child on her lap for much of the process. Finally, I want to acknowledge my children Noah, Seth, and Willow. They will face greater challenges and opportunities in their careers than I ever did, and I wish them satisfaction, joy, peace, and success.

PREFACE

The world has changed dramatically since I began my career in 1958. Most of the changes have been for the good. Unquestionably, the world is much more chaotic and volatile. But on the plus side, new industries, technologies, and challenges are springing up more rapidly than ever before. This creates new jobs before people can even train specifically for them. It also creates terrific opportunities for those who are ready. This book exists to make you ready.

On the challenging side, economic shocks, scandals, global competition, and government intervention cause greater uncertainty than ever before. Jobs are destroyed and created more rapidly than ever. Businesses and even entire industries come and go. New competitors spring up from around the world—armed with cost advantages, technological advantages, and talented employees. The government gets involved more than in the past. Economic shocks and scandals seem to come more rapidly. We have to be ready for whatever comes next.

In this environment people need to be agile. They need to be ready to shift from employee to entrepreneur, freelancer, interim executive, investor, student, sabbatical taker, and more.

People need to create a bulletproof career by having great relationships—a power base—and also by constantly upgrading their skills. That way they can get into the opportunity flow, and opportunities *will* come their way.

People need a mindset that encourages resilience, improvisation, and street smarts.

Everyone should be thinking about the opportunities and threats that can affect one's career, both inside and outside the organization. Then they need to be ready to adapt, with an open mind as well as with flip-the-switch backup plans that can be implemented immediately if an ambush threatens.

The Guerrilla Marketing philosophy is perfect in this environment. Given how quickly things change, this philosophy—which used to apply mainly to small business owners—now applies to employees, entrepreneurs, and everyone in between. It has been a hallmark of my own career—as an advertising agency executive and then as an author and speaker.

Andrew Neitlich is the perfect person to write this book with me. He is very open about the ways his career has meandered as he tried to find the ideal match among his passions, talents, and market opportunities. He graduated from Harvard Business School, after turning down Harvard Law School. He worked on Wall Street, in government, for both large and small companies, and finally—just over a decade ago—he launched a successful career as a consultant and entrepreneur. He has faced failures, such as a losing business venture in the professional fight-promotion business. He has also had many successes and is now a successful and highly regarded Internet publisher, trainer, consultant, author, and executive-level coach.

As I have, Andrew has crafted an ideal life for himself. He works from his home office, plays tennis as often as he likes, and has plenty of time to spend with his wife and children. This book is a compilation of his own experiences, as well as those of his colleagues, family, friends, and thousands of people from around the world he has trained and coached over the past decade.

As one who has worked from his home—a three-day week at that—and earned far more than I possibly could have as an employee, I resonate with all the ideas presented here.

I hope you are ready for the enlightenment that Andrew provides in these pages.

Jay Conrad Levinson
DeBary, Florida

INTRODUCTION
Opportunities in Perpetually
Gut-Wrenching Times —
for Guerrillas Only!

T here is nowhere to hide. The economy can be sizzling, flat, or in a recession. You can own a business, work for someone else, be a college professor, or work in government. It doesn't matter where in the world you live and work, whether you telecommute or work in an office, or whether you work full-time or part-time.

At any minute you can face an ambush that can turn your career upside down.

If you lived through the dot-com bubble and the Great Recession of 2008–10, you know this. You remember Enron, which in its time was seen as a model of the new Internet age, before it collapsed under scandal and house-of-cards accounting tricks. When it fell, thousands of employees lost their jobs, pensions, and what they thought was a guaranteed retirement. Andersen Consulting, the big-five accounting firm that imploded because of its auditing relationship and practices with Enron, cost thousands more people their jobs—even if those people didn't directly work with Enron. During the same era, people experienced the rapid disappearance of large and small Internet companies, along with the millions of dollars in stock options that so many employees thought they had in the bank.

During the Great Recession, the unemployment rate hit 9.7 percent in the USA. True unemployment, which counts people who stop looking for a job as well as workers who are forced to work part-time, reached 17.5 percent by March, 2010. The average time between jobs reached as high as thirty-one weeks. Entire industries—automotive, banking, construction, and real estate—nearly collapsed. While too-big-to-fail businesses got bailed out, Main Street businesses faced an unprecedented credit crunch. Many business owners lost everything because they couldn't hold out until good times returned. A Google search of layoffs during this time reveals dozens of stories of employees from all sectors—business, government, and nonprofit—using words like shocked and blindsided to describe their reaction to their sudden layoff.

Even in good times, no one can count on stability. Jobs get outsourced. New technologies eliminate old jobs while creating entirely new ones, jobs that may require entirely new qualifications. Foreign competitors win market share over local companies with lower costs. Mergers cut positions as companies come together and eliminate redundancy. Investors push for cost cuts, a.k.a. layoffs, to assure a strong quarterly earnings report. Government gets involved in an industry, which often makes it harder for employers in that industry to retain top talent or compete. A scandal breaks and jobs disappear, even if the affected employees are many departments and layers removed from the executives who caused the problem in the first place. Consumer tastes change, and a company's products fall out of favor. A product liability lawsuit, even one without merit, causes major damage to the company's reputation along with profit write-downs and layoffs. An employee doesn't get along with his or her boss or with an influential colleague and gets pushed aside or out.

It really is a jungle out there. Uncertainty is everywhere and you have to be prepared for sudden ambushes. It is time for a new set of rules—guerrilla rules—to survive and thrive.

Take a moment to consider what you would do if you knew that in six months you would lose your job, or—if you own a business—your company would collapse. What would you do now to prepare? What if you knew that in three months you would lose your current job or business? One month? Tomorrow? What if you got the call right now? Many people would be like cows in line for slaughter, even if they were self-aware cows who knew what was going to happen to them when they reached the front of the line. They'd feel scared, they'd complain with loud moos, they'd hope for the best, but they'd still move forward in line as each cow in front of them is killed. What about you? Are you ready to flip a switch and earn income in other ways, or are you like a cow in line for slaughter?

This book is not for cows. It is for guerrillas. The goal of this book is to help you bulletproof your career, avoid career ambushes, and succeed in spite of perpetually gut-wrenching and uncertain times. I want you to leave this book 100 percent ready for combat: prepared to advance your career and take care of your family without ever being blindsided by overnight industry collapses, layoffs, economic shocks, corporate scandals, government intervention, or technological disruptions. I want you to never again have to worry about financial peace of mind or job security, because you will have a new set of strategies for success in a volatile and continuously evolving economy. This applies equally to business owners who need to plan for extreme volatility in the market and who recognize that their careers will likely extend beyond owning a single company, and to employees who can lose their jobs at almost any time.

The time to prepare is NOW—not when you face a career crisis, not when you need a new job, and not when you are out of cash. If you follow the tactics and strategies in this book, you will have the relationships, skills, and resources you need to get the first shot at opportunities. You will be prepared with backup plans in case bad news affects your current career situation. You will protect everything you have worked so hard to achieve in your career so far, while advancing and making more money with less effort.

The book has four parts. Part I prepares you for combat. It shows you how to take your talents, dreams, and network and move into the opportunity flow. That way, opportunities come your way, and you don't have to chase them. Part II shows you the perspectives to be savvy as you find, evaluate, and negotiate opportunities. Part III gives you a variety of options for earning an income and being agile throughout your career. The focus is on providing value rather than being attached to the obsolete concept of a job. Note that this part of the book applies equally to business owners, because the lifespan of a typical business virtually guarantees that most entrepreneurs will play many roles during their work life. Part IV concludes with some common yet challenging situations that many of us face during our careers, and information on how to handle them.

The book doesn't end there. Please visit the Web site that accompanies this book, www.bulletproofcareer.com. This Web site is a special resource created specifically for readers of this book to get additional information, tools, research, advice, podcasts, and support. This resource is included with the price of the book and costs nothing more, so why not take advantage of it?

Despite the potential risks and pitfalls in today's economy, there is a tremendous upside if you embrace the guerrilla philosophy and tactics. Never before have there been so many different ways to earn an income and contribute to others. If you are agile and resilient, you can have wonderful adventures throughout your career, along with constant learning, increased flexibility, and freedom. You can work from wherever you want and with whomever you want. You can start a company, sell it, work as an executive at the acquiring company, and then start yet another company or invest in other entrepreneurs. You can be a solopreneur working with many clients and choosing your own hours and projects. You can be an interim executive, working hard six months and then relaxing six months. Of course, if you prefer having a traditional job, you can keep advancing from one job to another with greater ease than most of your peers. That's because you have solid relationships with people in the know, people who keep you informed of opportunities before they get posted publicly. It is up to you, and, for guerrillas, the opportunities are almost limitless.

PART I:

GET

COMBAT-READY

outside circumstances could eliminate your position or reduce your influence at any time.

There are very few reasons to stay loyal to an employer. The first reason is that the company provides you with a clear, explicit, believable path to get rich. For instance, you work at a major investment bank, your employment contract includes a golden parachute that pays you handsomely if you leave, you receive already-registered stock options in a publicly traded, growing company, and/or your career path has been proven to make others rich within five to seven years. The second reason is that the company gives you incredible ways to tap into your passion, learn, develop, and set yourself up for future opportunities while building relationships with talented, high-profile people who can help you throughout your career. If these things are not in place in your job, or you sense that they are slipping away, prepare to make a change.

Even if you love your job, you absolutely, positively need a backup plan in order to stay in control of your career. You need relationships and a documented track record to quickly find a new position, and you should be ready to earn income via forms other than full-time employment. The time to put this foundation in place is NOW, not when you get ambushed.

Most importantly, and to repeat what you read above: give up the idea that a formal, full-time job is the only acceptable way for you to make a living.

A full-time job is not necessarily the best way to earn an income, make a contribution to others, and achieve your dreams. True guerrillas understand this and are prepared to provide value to others through many different forms.

Instead, think about how you can best bring your unique gifts, talents, and contributions to others—regardless of the formal legal description of how you do your work. Change is so unpredictable and can come so quickly that you need to be ready to adapt at any time. You need to be able to flip the switch from employee to freelancer to sabbatical-taker, back to employee, to interim executive to entrepreneur to student to expatriate in an unfamiliar country to investor to retiree, back to employee, and so on. The most adaptable and agile people will experience the greatest career success with the fewest setbacks and be the least likely to feel like victims during tough times.

You probably know lots of people whose careers have meandered from one of the above forms to the other and then perhaps back again. You may be such a person, or will be soon. I definitely am. As I think about my own friends, colleagues, and family members, I can't think of many who haven't experienced somewhat chaotic and ever-morphing career paths. In some cases, they build on previous experiences and skills. In others, they start again from scratch. A very small sample includes:

- **Fired from first job and then starts up a venture fund.** After a college graduate got fired from his first job, he immediately moved to Hong Kong, despite having no background in or significant knowledge of Chinese culture. He learned Mandarin and worked for a telecommunications and cable company for a few years. Then he returned to the United States to get his MBA and now runs a successful venture fund focused on Asian business.

- **An attorney born and raised in the United States moves to Australia to become a veterinarian.** A frustrated lawyer from Florida relocated to Sydney, Australia, to study veterinary medicine. He chose Australia because entrance requirements were less stringent than in the United States. His wife, an emergency medicine physician, went with him. She got licensed to practice medicine in Australia and now works for the emergency room of a hospital in Sydney. The couple is thrilled to be living in Sydney and can't see moving back to the United States anytime soon.

- **Displaced executive in the family business becomes a mental health therapist.** When an executive got kicked out of his family's manufacturing business, he decided to get his PhD in mental health therapy. Now he runs a successful therapy practice while also teaching psychology at an online university and tutoring students online for extra income.

- **Artist turns Internet entrepreneur.** A former full-time artist worked as a wine sommelier in a four-star restaurant, started up a nanny placement agency, taught kids tae kwon do, and worked with kids in a nonprofit arts organization. After becoming a stay-at-home mom, she combined all of these experiences by launching an award-winning online product company offering parenting tools, etiquette curricula, and arts-and-crafts curricula for mothers and teachers. You will read more about her in a later chapter.

- **High school teacher becomes a millionaire leadership communications expert.** A high school teacher started a nonprofit theater company for kids. After a decade dealing with the challenges of fundraising and managing a board of directors, he capitalized on his directing skills in a big way. In his spare time, he led workshops about how to communicate with impact based on the techniques that top actors and theater directors use to create award-winning performances. A business seminar company liked his approach and invited him to lead seminars for their clients, including Global 2000 corporations. From there he has built a million-dollar consulting practice training corporate executives to communicate more powerfully.

What about you? What twists and turns has your career already taken? What are the possible shapes your career will take in the next few years and beyond? What do you want to happen? What circumstances outside your control could force you to scramble for new opportunities? What is the best that can happen, if you really dream big? What might go wrong? What backup plans might you need in place in order to be prepared? How can you build on your skills and relationships to reinvent yourself on the spot and take advantage of new opportunities? Later chapters will challenge you to go into more depth with your answers so that you shift from thinking about the issues to taking proactive action.

It is daunting to face so much uncertainty and so many possible shifts. As the next chapter explains, you need a rare and special set of attitudes.

CHAPTER 2

THE ELEVEN GUERRILLA MINDSETS
FOR CAREER SUCCESS

I t takes mental toughness to be prepared for today's economic climate. Nothing short of a guerrilla mindset will do. Following are eleven guerrilla mindsets that you must embrace in order to be combat-ready in today's economy. Once you incorporate these attitudes into your life and let them guide your actions, the odds increase significantly that wonderful opportunities will come your way.

As you consider these mindsets, remember that you and you alone create your own attitude in your career and life. While external circumstances can be challenging, they don't dictate your internal state. You do. At any time you can proactively generate the mindset you need to remain resilient, fearless, and able to see possibilities. You alone control the ability to keep moving forward in the face of obstacles. You are always in control of your own state of mind—even if the road is longer or harder than you had expected, even if no one else believes in you, even if unanticipated obstacles get in your way. Don't be a victim. Don't let any automatic and negative patterns of thoughts and feelings get in your way. Create the mental state you need to be proactive, tough, and ready to take on whatever comes your way.

Guerrilla Mindset One: Provide value. Getting it done, doing lots of tasks, and spending lots of time is not sufficient for guerrillas. What matters is getting results that serve others by bringing significant value to them and to their organizations. How much value? Think about generating ten times your fees or salary. If you make $100,000 a year, you had better be adding $1,000,000 in value. Otherwise, you are at risk.

If you embrace this attitude alone and none of the others to follow, you might change your entire career focus. For instance, many information technology professionals are great at developing work plans and following them to the letter. However, studies show that fewer than 10 percent of information technology

By the way, taking 100 percent responsibility will immediately set you apart in a world that seems more focused than ever on bailouts, complaining, blaming others, and being a victim.

Guerrilla Mindset Six: Be completely professional. True professionals bring an attitude of service, integrity, and even refinement to everything they do. They set the highest standards and constantly raise them. Professionals have clients while the rest of us have customers.

Likewise, professionals have a practice, while the rest of us have jobs or businesses. Practice is an interesting word. It refers not only to a professional's business, but also to the hard work that top performers do every day in order to improve their skills continuously and remain at the top of their game.

What if you thought of your career as a professional practice in that sense, even if you aren't in a field that traditionally uses that description? What if you thought of everyone as a client or potential client, a relationship worthy of trust, respect, and long-term mutual benefit? Imagine how you could set yourself apart from peers who don't embody the same professionalism and focus on personal relationships.

Guerrilla Mindset Seven: Constantly learn and improve. If you cultivate this attitude, you will never let yourself stagnate. You will constantly seek new opportunities to develop, sharpen your capabilities, and improve your performance. As soon as you feel comfortable, recognize that it's time to take your expertise to another level. You seek mastery and realize that mastery is a never-ending journey.

At a practical level, you are open to feedback and advice from others. When you get tough advice, you don't get defensive or take offense. Instead, you consider whether the feedback is true and is something that can help you improve.

Guerrilla Mindset Eight: See what is possible and move things forward, especially when others won't. When others are depressed, negative, apathetic, or cynical, you see new possibilities to move forward. You are not unrealistic, but you are optimistic and proactive. You constantly find ways to move people toward results. If people get stuck overanalyzing, you nudge them to make a decision, knowing that complete information does not exist. If people refuse to take action, you diplomatically challenge them to commit. If people go a bit off-track, you help them adjust course and resume progress before it is too late to recover. The same is true in your own career. You constantly create new possibilities and opportunities, whether on your current track or while reinventing yourself.

Guerrilla Mindset Nine: Show courage and determination even in the face of fear. We are born with only two fears hardwired into our brains: a fear of heights, and a fear of loud noises. Soon we learn to fear things that cause us physical harm and pain. Then, as we grow, the mind takes over and somehow trains us to be fearful of all manner of imaginary problems.

The guerrilla recognizes that most of our fears are not real. Even if you feel fear while navigating your career, have the courage to get through whatever comes your way. You prepare yourself ahead of time so that you are ready to handle especially difficult career challenges. You are not afraid of being fired, because you have relationships and backup plans ready to go at any time, and because you live within your means in case your financial situation changes quickly. You are not afraid of losing business or a client, because you have marketing systems in place to get new business. You are not afraid of uncertainties and circumstances outside your control, because you anticipate risks and are ready for whatever comes your way. Even if bad things happen or it takes longer than you thought it would to get back on track, you persevere.

You are also determined and courageous when it comes to advancing your career. You don't take irresponsible risks like an impulsive gambler, but you are willing to seek out new opportunities to advance and achieve your goals. Similarly, you ask the people in your network for help and reach out to new people whom you should know—even if it makes you nervous to do so. Unlike most people in the world, you don't hide behind someday; you have the courage to take action and make things happen, even if you fail a few times, or more.

Guerrilla Mindset Ten: Be inspired. You are passionate and inspired by what you are trying to achieve in your career. Unlike most people, you realize that inspiration comes from within, not from anything outside you. You are able to tap into that place within you that is filled with natural enthusiasm for what you are doing. You are working for something that gets you excited, nurtures and sustains you, contributes to the greater good, and fills you with gratitude. Your inspiration doesn't have to show up as charisma, mania, or fake motivation, like those people who seem to try too hard to smile all the time. It is more like a slow-burning flame. As long as you have that inspiration, good things tend to follow. When times get tough, you have the energy to keep going forward and to eventually succeed when others give up. Even better, your inspiration is infectious; you naturally inspire others and thereby attract all sorts of helpful resources and high-profile people your way.

Guerrilla Mindset Eleven: Have fun. The stakes are high in any career. We work to provide for our needs, take care of our families, and be somebody in life. However, that's no reason to be so intense and serious in your career that you let the rest of life pass you by. Take your career seriously and, at the same time, enjoy the ride. Cultivate a lightness of spirit. Keep your sense of humor. When you do, you instantly become more likeable. More people will want you on the team and will want to help you succeed.

CHAPTER 3

CHARACTER AND VALUES
MATTER MORE THAN EVER

iven the huge numbers of well-publicized business scandals over the past years, from Enron to bonuses on Wall Street to Bernie Madoff's historic Ponzi scheme, people feel cynical toward big business and business executives. For this reason, employers, investors, and customers place greater value than ever on people with unquestioned integrity. It is a simple matter of supply and demand. Character and values have become disappointingly uncommon and therefore increasingly precious. In other words, authentic character and values give you an edge, especially in chaotic times.

Character is a measure of your moral and ethical integrity. It means having the courage to seek out and do what is right, even if you have incentives, like keeping your job or making a big commission, to do what is wrong. Values are the principles that matter most to you and define your character.

In business, integrity sits on an extremely slippery slope. One minute you are doing the right thing and then, perhaps even before you consider the potential consequences, you start cutting some important corners. Once you start making small ethical infractions, it gradually becomes easier to violate more serious ethical codes. If you lose your moral compass, you risk finding yourself engaged in morally reprehensible behavior that may have a devastating impact on others.

This happened during the mortgage boom that started around 2002 and lasted until the housing bust of 2008. As competition grew in the mortgage industry, mortgage brokers started using more and more devious tactics to close deals. Some mortgage brokers altered client pay stubs to make a loan appear less risky. They encouraged clients to lie about their income on stated income loans, promising that "this is what it takes to get the loan done, and banks expect it." Some appraisers, especially those with cozy relationships with mortgage firms, changed the facts about a home's features to arrive at an appraised value that a bank would accept. Thanks to these practices, it will take a long time for this industry to recover trust and credibility.

In this kind of environment, character and integrity are platinum. For instance, one major public university had an admissions scandal that led to the resignation of the president along with many members of the board of trustees. The remaining trustees chose as the interim president a tenured professor and department head at the university who was known for having impeccable integrity. He was the perfect person to lead the university out of crisis. Similarly, I know an entrepreneur who was able to get $300,000 in unsecured financing for a business venture. He was a gifted entrepreneur but his investors gave him better than usual terms because he had developed a reputation for integrity in all of his previous business dealings.

How would you rate your character and integrity? When have you walked away from a shady business deal or practice? When have you done the wrong thing in order to finesse a business deal or result? How many people do you know who would lend you $300,000 or more unsecured, based on your character?

Only you know for sure, and I hope you have the courage to do a truthful assessment. Regardless, two things are clear. First, if you do something wrong, others will find out. If the smartest swindlers in the world, like Bernie Madoff, can't get away with their schemes forever, no one can. If you indulge in questionable business practices, you will be caught. And secondly, once you start down that road, it is easier to keep going than to turn back. But if you are wise, you will never take that first step. Take a moment and consider any behaviors or business practices you must curtail right now.

Part of your character includes the values you hold dear. Your values define the principles and attributes you expect from a company, colleague, employee, employer, or business partner. These values tell you where you want to work, the way you want to work, and, more importantly, where and how you *don't* want to work. They also give you substance, so that you come across to others as a person with a strong moral foundation.

What are your top values? For instance, a colleague of mine has always valued fair treatment of employees. At one point in his career, he took an executive position with a cable company. He quickly discovered that the executives there enjoyed wonderful perquisites at the company, while front-line employees were treated like serfs. He couldn't stomach the huge disparity in pay and benefits at the top compared to what the people serving customers on the front lines got. Realizing his mistake, he left the company and his hefty paycheck, even though he had no new job in place. That's character!

Take a moment to list the top five values you have and expect from any business opportunity, job, business partner, or company. A lengthy list of possibilities includes: adaptability, accountability, achievement, adventure, agility, amazement, balance, caring, caution, challenge, collegiality, commitment, community, competitiveness, contribution, control, courage, creativity, customer-focus, cutting edge, dignity, diversity, enthusiasm, entrepreneurial spirit, environmental awareness, ethics, fairness, flexibility, focus, free time, growth, harmony, honesty, humor, independence, initiative, innovation, integrity, intelligence, justice, leadership, learning, listening, long-term perspective, loyalty, making a difference, mission, money, peace, power, prestige, quality, recognition, relationships, relaxation, reliability, resilience, respect, responsibility, results, risk, safety, service, spirituality, status, success, teamwork, tolerance, toughness, tradition, trust, unity, variety, vision, wealth, winning, wisdom, and wonder.

Which values, whether from the above or your own list, are non-negotiable for you? At the same time, what are negative values you won't tolerate from anyone or any organization?

The more you live with integrity and a core set of values, the easier it becomes to find opportunities that fit who you are. It also becomes easier to attract like-minded people who open up new opportunities for you.

Please give this chapter its due! Character and values are not fluff. Take them seriously. The world needs people with character and values more than ever before.

CHAPTER 4

A DREAM WORTH FIGHTING FOR

A s you prepare to get combat-ready, keep asking yourself this question: Am I pursuing a dream worth fighting for?

Even with an economy in constant flux and with risks around every corner, you have every right to seek a worthy dream. In fact, you need a dream *in spite* of all of this uncertainty. A worthy dream inspires you and keeps you going during tough times. It gives you the energy you need to keep pushing forward.

However, it has to be *your* dream. The world is constantly pushing dreams on you. Your parents, siblings, friends, boyfriends or girlfriends, teachers, movies, television, celebrities, and religious groups: they all have points of view about what makes the good life. Don't let the world tell you who or what you need to be. Figure it out for yourself.

It's not an easy quest. Many successful people in their forties and fifties look back and wonder what happened. They did everything they were supposed to do. They went to the right schools, got the right jobs, married the right spouse, and lived in the right places. But they aren't happy. What happened is that they signed up for somebody else's dream and it came up empty for them.

You are going to die, maybe tomorrow, maybe in a few decades. Only you can decide what pursuits will have made your time worthy. Only you can find the best match among your talents, passions, values, and viable ways to earn a living. There is no single way to figure it out, and there are never guarantees. As the old adage warns, "Be careful what you wish for." Some people know at age six what they want to do for the rest of their lives, and they make it happen. Others meander around for years figuring out what they like and don't like, and eventually something clicks for them. Still others go from achieving one dream to another every few years, enjoying fantastic adventures along the way. Unfortunately, far too many people never find their calling, are unwilling to be fulfilled no matter what they do, or lack the courage to take action to create a life and career they adore.

While the answers can take a lifetime to come by, the questions alone are worthy of your time:

- What are the core values that define how you want to live and the work you want to do?

- What are the core values that are the opposite of how you want to live and work?

- What types of activities inspire you? What types of activities do you dislike?

- Where do you want to live? Where do you *not* want to live?

- What kind of lifestyle do you want to have? What kind of lifestyle do you *not* want to have?

- What do you want your workday to be like? What do you want your workday *not* to be like?

- What contribution do you want to make to others, and why will this nurture you?

- With what kinds of people do you want to work? With what kinds of people do you *not* want to work?

- Which talents do you have and want to use? Which talents do you have that you do *not* enjoy using?

- Which occupations do you admire? Which do you *not* admire?

- What are family, friends, and society telling you that you should do in your career, even though you don't want to? What are they telling you that you shouldn't do in your career, even though you want to and think you would be successful?

- What is a hobby you love that you would love to turn into a career, assuming you could make a living doing it?

- Who are people you admire, and how might their lives inspire your career choice?

- If you could live anywhere, where would it be? What would it take for you to live there, if you don't already?

- How important is family to you? How might family priorities influence your career dreams?

- What is your vision of an ideal world, and what career choices could help you to make your vision a reality?

- What is your vision for yourself and what you want to be doing in five, ten, and twenty years?

- What achievements would make the next five years worthy? Ten years? Fifty years?

- If you had a magic wand that could do anything, how would you use it to create the ideal career for you?

- Knowing that there is no magic wand and that there are rarely ideal situations, what are the negatives and potential downsides of your dream career? Examples include dealing with long hours and little or no social life, living somewhere you don't want to live your whole life, wearing suits, doing low-level work for a while, or working for peanuts. Are you willing and able to tolerate these downsides?

- What are things that will get in the way of your taking immediate action and small steps to achieve your dream?

If you struggle to answer the above questions, consider working with a career coach who can help you explore and develop your own dream. A good coach will have assessment tools and resources that can give you insights about your natural traits and talents. You can also find a list of assessment tools at www. bulletproofcareer.com. If you can't afford a coach, find a friend you trust who is willing to listen and work through the above questions with you. Alternatively, form a small group of friends who meet to discuss and share ideas about the above questions.

Even when you think you have found a dream worthy of your time and life's energy, you still need the courage to take action and turn your vision into reality. Nothing is more pathetic than a person who claims to be pursuing a dream but does nothing but talk about it. That's not a problem for the guerrilla. What is one step you can take right now to move you closer to your dream? Before you read further in this book, take that step!

CHAPTER 5

SPIKE IN THESE TWO AREAS AND NEVER WORRY AGAIN

What if you could be indispensable as you pursue your dream career? What if, in the face of a layoff at your company, the leadership team wouldn't even consider eliminating your position? What if, even after a major career failure or setback, the people in your industry still perceive you as a valuable and talented asset? What if you could get an ongoing stream of calls from recruiters, investors, and dealmakers offering you top-notch opportunities? Even better, what if decision-makers called you *first* whenever they had a new opportunity that fit your abilities?

You can make this happen. In fact, in order to have long-term career success and to achieve your most inspiring dreams, you *must* make this happen.

What you need to do is excel, or spike, in two areas. The first area where you should spike is with a technical or functional expertise that brings significant value to others and that you do better than just about anyone else. Excelling at a technical skill generally requires advanced education and study in fields such as engineering, medicine, materials science, software development, architecture, and biotechnology. If you choose to spike in a functional skill, you need to demonstrate a track record of results in areas like managing a business unit, finance, marketing, sales, accounting, human resources, law, strategy, and negotiation.

The second area in which to spike is in relationships with relevant decision-makers and opinion-leaders. Depending on your career aspirations, these people include leaders in your chosen industry and function—investors, recruiters, professionals with skills that are complementary to your own, and people with connections who can help you succeed.

Take a look at the grid below, which illustrates these two spikes:

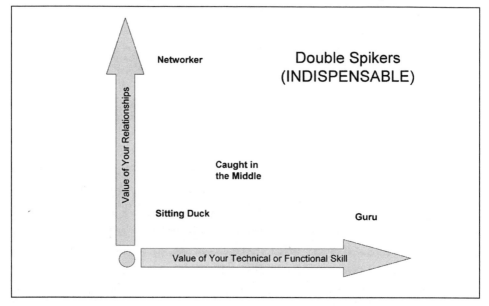

The Sitting Duck, lower left corner. The Sitting Duck is someone without a valued technical skill and without valuable relationships. You are temporarily a Sitting Duck when you start out in your career or make a transition into a completely new field. You could be a permanent Sitting Duck if you happen to be lazy, unmotivated, or just not paying attention to what counts in today's career marketplace. If you are a sitting duck, you have a long way to go and lots to do before you become indispensable.

Caught in the Middle. Most people are Caught in the Middle, even if they don't want to admit it. They have decent technical or functional skill, but they haven't separated themselves from the pack. They have some relationships, but aren't in with the key decision-makers in their function or industry. If you are caught in the middle, you need to do two things. First, you have to work hard to develop your technical or functional skills in ways that wow people with your ability to get results and create value. Second, build relationships with more people who matter.

The Guru, lower right corner. The Guru has incredible technical or functional skills but few high-powered relationships. Imagine the brilliant but introverted computer software expert. While he may be secure in a current position, he is vulnerable. In fact, he probably can't stand the fact that less qualified people who happen to have better relationships sometimes get opportunities he never even hears about. The Guru usually does fine over the life of his career as word spreads about his expertise, but he could do even better if he developed a stronger network of relationships.

The Networker, upper left corner. As the name suggests, the Networker has a large sphere of influence. He can use this network of contacts to open up opportunities for himself while also connecting others to opportunities. However, he is vulnerable, although for the opposite reason that the Guru is. The Networker's challenge is to improve his expertise and ability to get substantive results. That way, he can bring greater and greater value to his power base and remain credible.

For instance, I know one Networker, a former professional basketball player, who has more than three thousand names in his Rolodex. He didn't make enough money to retire on while playing sports, and he is thinking about ways to earn a living now that his playing days have ended. His strategy is to learn everything he can about insurance and financial products so that he can parlay his network of contacts into a source of income and a second career.

Double Spikers, upper right corner. Finally, Double Spikers are career superstars. These are the people who get called first and can dictate their own terms. They have both the valuable skills and the network. Barring a scandal, they are pretty much unstoppable. For instance, I work with a banker who spent his career at top investment banks, doing deals in emerging technology companies. He has proven that he has an eye for spotting outstanding investment opportunities in this sector. At the same time, his reputation is spotless. He has worked with and earned the respect of some of the top financiers and entrepreneurs in the industry. Now he works from his home office in Florida while screening dozens of opportunities every week to invest in dynamic companies. He doesn't have to do anything to get access to these deals except check his e-mail and answer his phone. The people in his network know the kinds of deals he seeks, and they send high-quality opportunities his way. He is the perfect example of somebody who combines valuable, functional expertise with a strong network.

You can use the professional social-networking Web site LinkedIn (www. linkedin.com) to identify Double Spikers.

These are people with impressive resumes and high-profile contacts. For instance, one of my LinkedIn contacts has a history of successful leadership positions in the metals and mining industry. He has been a CIO, COO, and CEO at billion-dollar companies in this industry. When you look at his connections on LinkedIn, almost all of them are also CEOs and top-tier professionals from within his field, along with leading business executives in his home city. At this point in his career, this gentleman is leading his own coaching and consulting firm while mentoring CEOs of mid-sized companies. He is always one call away from CEOs in his industry and is extremely well-connected in the business community where he lives.

Similarly, a friend of mine who leads marketing and sales teams for software companies just got laid off from his most recent job. However, he is not worried, even in a very difficult economy. "I am considering five different opportunities and should be employed again within the month," he shared with me. He has this many options because he is well-connected in his industry and has a track record of results. His network of contacts opened doors for him. His track record of results will close the deal. Because he is a Double Spiker, he gets access to opportunities before they are posted and gets offers because of his proven ability to create value.

Take a moment to consider your own career. Where do you fall on the grid? Start with your technical/functional value. What would you need to do to become a true guru in your field? How does that compare to where you are now? What assignments, people, training, and education can help you get to where you need to be? What can you do NOW to take a step forward?

What about the value of your relationships? Who are the key people in your function and industry? Who controls the money? Who makes the major decisions? Who sets opinion? Who makes the biggest deals? Who has power with the government? How well-connected are you to these people? What will it take for you to reach Networker status? What can you do NOW to meet more of these people, or improve your relationships with them?

If you find yourself Caught in the Middle or are a Sitting Duck, take comfort. Assuming that you are willing to work hard, your progress accelerates over time. New, more challenging assignments and achievements introduce you to new people. These people make connections for you from their network, which can lead to new assignments. If you remain focused on building relevant relationships while also improving your expertise, your career will spiral upward into Double Spiker territory and indispensable status.

The experience of a colleague who used to work for me illustrates the way a career can accelerate quickly. After college, he worked as a project assistant for a direct marketing company. He became competent at placing advertisements, managing customer communications, and creating reports about marketing campaign results. What would translate into great news for him was that he lacked a pedigree from an Ivy League school. His employer, who perhaps cared a bit too much about that kind of thing, refused to promote him to a management role. After almost a decade working for this company, he felt like he was beginning to stagnate and started reaching out to vendors and recruiters in the industry. When a recruiter called him about a management position at a major direct marketing firm, he jumped at the opportunity. He performed spectacularly in his new job while also taking leadership roles in industry associations and continuing to build relationships with top vendors, entrepreneurs, and experts. A few years later, in his early thirties, he became the CEO of a multi-million dollar online publishing company. His network now includes the equivalent of a Who's Who in the industry, and his expertise is widely respected. After almost a decade languishing in a dead-end role, he took matters into his own hands and now earns more money and has more responsibility than most of the pedigreed MBAs he left behind in his old company.

Meanwhile, a colleague I'll call Nelson provides an example of someone who started with no knowledge or relationships in an industry and found success within two years. Facing a career crisis after being laid off as an accountant, he thought back to the paper mills near his childhood home and the way that they fascinated him while he was growing up. He decided that he would become the expert who knew more about the paper industry than anyone else. He approached an investment bank and asked if he could join the bank to make deals in the paper industry. The bank gave him an office, a phone, and a commission-only salary structure. Nelson had to eat what he killed or go hungry. Within two years of making calls, meeting the key players, and learning the ropes of investment banking through self-study, he developed a thriving investment banking practice.

You can achieve the same success in whichever field you choose. It takes time and discipline, because you have to focus intently on building up a valuable expertise you enjoy while also building important relationships. However, if you spend your energy on these two pursuits, it won't take long to pass by your less ambitious colleagues who are Caught in the Middle and can't figure out why their careers are stuck.

CHAPTER 6

CREATE YOUR ONE-PAGE CAREER PLAN

A useful way to keep your career goals in the forefront of your mind is by creating your one-page career plan. The one-page career plan is a living, breathing, dynamic document that helps you focus on where you are headed and what you need to do to get there. Whether you are a student, employee, freelancer, or entrepreneur, the one-page career plan helps you think about how to keep improving and moving forward. It turns your career into a project and helps you define the things you need to do to get where you want to be.

Take some time to fill in your own plan, using the template at the end of this chapter and the following instructions as a guide:

The area of expertise where you will spike. Write down the one functional or technical area where you will set yourself apart from others. Examples:

- I will be the leading expert in etiquette training.
- I know more about economic pricing elasticity models than anyone else.
- I will be an expert in building and selling software development firms.
- I will be the leading wedding photographer on the Gulf Coast of Florida.
- I will be the top human resource executive for professional services firms.

The specific, measurable value you bring to others. Describe the results you get for others that make you indispensable and make your worth ten times your salary or fees. For instance:

- My etiquette-training packages show stay-at-home moms how to build a business while preparing kids for a solid future. I charge $200 per package and my customers can build a $30,000 per year part-time business with my information.

- My pricing models help companies maximize their revenues and profits by pricing their products exactly right. A $200,000 engagement can easily add $2 million to a company's bottom line.

- I create companies from scratch that can be worth $5 million or more, usually within five years.

- My customers cherish their wedding photos for a lifetime and proudly display them in their homes.

- With my help, professional service firms attract and retain the best talent in the industry.

Your vision of what you want to achieve in your career. Write down your major goals, including the lifestyle that your career allows you to have down the road.

- I am known as the leading etiquette trainer for modern times. I appear on national television shows and have a best-selling book. I make enough money to support my family. I stay home and take care of the kids. I play as much tennis as I want.

- Fortune 500 companies rely on my economic models. I charge $10,000 per day. I travel the world first-class while working with clients. I live in a home on Malibu.

- After selling my next company, I am a leading Silicon Valley venture capitalist and part-time instructor at Stanford Business School.

- I win the top awards in the photography world and my work is featured in major wedding and photography publications. I continue to work out of my home. People from all over the country call to hire me. My schedule is booked a year in advance. My fees are high enough that I can do photography part-time while fishing on my boat in the Gulf the rest of the time. I absolutely love my life!

- I lead the HR function of a Fortune 500 company, receiving enough stock options to retire comfortably within five years.

The top three to five values that guide your career. List the values that define who you are and how you will work, using the previous chapter as a guide. For instance:

- Being a great mom, loving my husband; quality, winning, and excellence
- Precision, professionalism, and integrity
- Competition, teamwork, open communication, and adventure
- Aesthetics, service, fun, and love
- Energy, enthusiasm, continuous learning, and creativity

The one to three most advantageous possible next steps in your career. What would be the best next steps for you? Think about immediate next steps as well as opportunities you will target over the next three to five years. The world moves so quickly that it is unrealistic to plan out moves beyond three to five years. Examples:

- Roll out a live protocol training seminar for executives. Create a certification program for teenagers. Hire a publicist to book me on radio and television shows.
- Target ten Fortune 500 companies as clients and reach out to them. Speak at an upcoming *Wall Street Journal* marketing conference. Publish an article about pricing strategies in *The Harvard Business Review*.
- Build my current company to $2 million in sales. Get to know the top venture capitalists in Silicon Valley. Join the local Angel Investment club.
- Get a position as the head of human resources for a multinational, top-tier management consulting firm like McKinsey, Bain, or Booz Allen.

The remainder of the one-page career plan focuses on your action plan. In order to achieve your career goals, you need to take action. The best ways to develop throughout your career include: taking on more challenging assignments and projects, acquiring new skills, developing relationships with the people who can help you succeed, and getting formal education and training that will move you forward. The one-page career plan gives you room to set some action goals and assign yourself a deadline.

Take the time you need to complete your one-page plan using the template on the next page. Show it to five people you trust, and get their advice. Once you are satisfied with it, post it somewhere where you see it every day, for instance on the bathroom mirror, next to your computer monitor, or on the refrigerator door.

The plan is never set in stone. You might discover new options. Your aspirations might change. The outlook for your organization, industry, or the economy as a whole might shift. Therefore, every month review your progress with the plan and update it. If you experience a setback, get off track, or aren't progressing as quickly as you would like, don't beat yourself up. Choose the action steps that will get you moving forward again.

One-Page Career Plan   **Date:**

The area of expertise where I will spike:		

The specific, measurable value I bring to others:		

My vision of what I want to achieve in my career:		

The top three to five values that guide my career:		

The one to three most advantageous possible next steps in my career:		

	What or Who	**By When**
The top one to three assignments, projects, or achievements I need in order to develop expertise and my track record:		
The top one to three key skills or knowledge I need to acquire:		
The top five mentors, industry leaders, functional experts, and other key people I need to know and don't know yet:		
Any specific formal education and training that will help me achieve my career vision:		
Other action steps that will help me achieve my career goals, vision, and next steps:		
Top one to three immediate next steps:		

Example: Author's One-Page Career Plan

(Note: Due to book size and format, the plan as shown requires two pages)

The area of expertise where I will spike:	
I will be a leading author, speaker, and consultant on career success.	

The specific, measurable value I bring to others:	
The people who follow my advice will never worry about financial security again and will find fulfillment and success in gut-wrenching times.	

My vision of what I want to achieve in my career:	
I work from home while serving dynamic, interesting clients from around the world. I travel internationally with my family to speak, consult, coach, and train.	

The top three to five values that guide my career:	
Variety, risk-taking, adventure, fun, and intellectual stimulation.	

The one to three most advantageous possible next steps in my career:	
Speak at major conferences, find international licensees for my training programs, and write the next book.	

	What or Who	By When
The top one to three assignments, projects, or achievements I need in order to develop expertise and my track record:	*Get signed as the keynote speaker at a major HR conference. Ditto for a major industry conference.*	*1/15 for first; 3/15 for the second.*
The top one to three key skills or knowledge I need to acquire:	*Work with a leading speaking coach to take my speaking to a new level of impact.*	*6/30*
The top five mentors, industry leaders, functional experts, and other key people I need to know, and don't know yet:	*Executive Director of US Chamber of Commerce, Executive Director of SHRM, Current US Labor Secretary, Florida Governor, CEO of IBM.*	*6/15*

	What or Who	By When
Any specific formal education and training that will help me achieve my career vision:	*Learn more about best practices in Search Engine Optimization and social networking for my Web sites.*	*3/25*
Other action steps that will help me achieve my career goals, vision, and next steps:	*Create a marketing plan for next year's sales that will double my income and revenue. Hire an intellectual property attorney to develop a licensing agreement for my intellectual property.*	*12/31*
Top one to three immediate next steps:	*Call speaking agent to get booked at next HR conference. Contact speaking coach. Start marketing plan.*	*This week!*

CHAPTER 7

WHY STRENGTHS ARE NOT ENOUGH—
What if You Have Distracting, Annoying, or Disturbing Behaviors and Don't Even Know It?

We all know people with distracting, annoying, or disturbing behaviors at work. The harder thing to recognize is whether you are one of them! If you are, chances are you don't even know it.

Dysfunctional behaviors can damage your career whether you are an employee or an entrepreneur. Nobody wants to work with an employee who is annoying, let alone help that person to advance in a company. Likewise, entrepreneurs with serious behavioral blind spots won't be able to keep top talent. They also risk alienating key customers, vendors, and investors. People with major behavioral issues and their companies are targets for lawsuits. They may face charges of creating a hostile work environment, tolerating sexual harassment, violating confidentiality, cooking the books, fraud, or myriad other complaints.

It is fashionable today to focus on one's strengths. Research, most notably by Marcus Buckingham and the Gallup Organization, shows that people are much more able to build on their strengths than to correct weaknesses. Therefore, the argument goes, put people in positions that are a fit with their natural strengths, and let them do what they do best.

That kind of thinking makes good sense. However, many people—and you may be one of them—have some serious behavioral issues that can keep them from achieving their career goals. Those issues must be dealt with immediately if you are to advance in your career or, at the very least, avoid losing ground.

Types of poor behavior range from bad etiquette all the way to downright unethical and illegal activities. Following are six categories of common problem behaviors. As you read about them, give some serious consideration to whether any apply to you.

Lack of etiquette. Etiquette gaffes at work come in many shapes and sizes: inappropriate dress that is too revealing, too casual, or sloppy; poor hygiene or grooming like bad breath, body odor, too much perfume, messy hair, too much makeup, and too much jewelry; annoying habits such as kicking against one's cubicle wall, typing too loudly, wearing squeaky shoes, habitually blowing one's nose or sniffling, hovering around other people's work spaces, eating aromatic foods at one's desk, and chewing loudly; not keeping promises by coming late to appointments and missing deadlines; and lacking general social grace, for example by not making eye contact, interrupting others, making cynical or snide comments, texting during meetings, breathing heavily or eating while on the phone, talking badly about others, giving too much personal information, gossiping, taking longer lunches than everyone else, leaving meetings before everyone is done, taking phone calls when someone is in your office, and showing a general feeling of entitlement compared to others.

Stress reaction: fight. You have probably heard of the biological fight or flight reaction. When we feel stress, we tend to either fight back or flee. These patterns can become automatic and pervasive, especially when we feel constant stress in the workplace. People who tend toward a fight reaction can get aggressive when under stress. Examples include: being arrogant, dismissing others, verbally abusing people in public, making rash decisions, blaming other people for mistakes, sabotaging others' work, lacking a sense of humor, refusing to admit mistakes or make amends, getting defensive during debates or conversations, taking offense at constructive feedback, hogging credit for a team effort, undermining others, and expecting other people to just get it done without support or guidance.

Stress reaction: flee. In contrast, those who tend to flee when they feel stress exhibit more avoidant, passive-aggressive behaviors. For instance, they might shy away from giving difficult feedback, let issues come to a boil before acting, make decisions too slowly, refuse to roll out anything until it is perfect, agree to things publicly and then fail to follow through, seek to be popular with employees rather than respected, tend to ramble rather than get to the point, and avoid conflicts wherever possible.

Failure to fit in. Some people hurt their careers because they can't or won't fit into an organization's culture and norms or constantly go against the grain. Being a maverick and risk-taker can be a good thing, but not when you go too far and come across as awkward, weird, or even obnoxious. Examples include: dressing eccentrically, coming across as awkward and uncomfortable during conversations or at meetings, refusing to socialize with coworkers, or ignoring procedures for no good reason. These types of people would rather be unique, individualistic, or self-righteous than successful.

Bad attitude. A guaranteed way to stall your career is by being cynical, apathetic, or negative: being disrespectful to your boss; saying derogatory things about your company or job as if you don't want to be there; doing the minimum work required to get by; not lending a hand to teammates or not asking how you can help; ignoring problems until they fester; or throwing up your hands when people come to you for help.

Unethical, illegal, and downright noxious behaviors. Finally, there are all kinds of behaviors that can ruin your career immediately and even put you in jail. Sexual harassment, discrimination, fraud, misleading investors, insider trading, putting workers in danger, knowingly shipping unsafe products, breaking environmental laws, breaking labor laws, and physically attacking a coworker all happen more often than they should. We see examples every day in the news, to the point where people are more cynical than ever about organizations and their leaders.

This type of behavior can even be part of your company culture. For instance, some hospitals still tolerate it when surgeons make lewd and abusive comments to nurses during surgery. The hospital leadership rationalizes, "After all, that's how surgeons have to blow off steam during high-pressure, life-and-death situations, right?" Wrong. Now hospitals are facing lawsuits and union grievances from nurses who refuse to tolerate this behavior any longer.

Unfortunately, the above behaviors don't come close to exhausting the range of annoying, dysfunctional, and unproductive things that go on in many organizations! We all have weaknesses and behaviors that aren't 100 percent productive, and some that are downright nasty. The question is whether these behaviors have consequences that will keep you from achieving your career goals.

To address these potential career-thwarters, you need the courage to discover your true impact on others—both positive and negative. Few people are willing to find out—and then accept—the potentially ugly truths about their behavior at work. If you have aspirations to keep moving up in your career, I strongly suggest you hire an executive coach. Your coach can interview your colleagues to learn more about how you come across to others, including your strengths and potential blind spots.

Alternatively, get a couple of trusted friends and colleagues to give you candid advice about any alarming behaviors or habits that you might have. Let them know that even if it might be hard for them to tell you that you have, for the sake of argument, an odor problem, you'd prefer to hear it from them first. It's better than hearing the same bad news from your boss during your performance review or being summoned by the HR director for an embarrassing private meeting.

Don't be that unfortunate employee who wonders why he never got promoted, or that would-be entrepreneur who couldn't raise funds just because he had an annoying habit that turned influential people off. Find out the truth about how you come across to others. Hopefully, what you learn will be easy to correct.

CHAPTER 8

ELIMINATE THE BIGGEST
REASON YOU WON'T SUCCEED

E veryone has at least one reason they won't succeed. What is yours?

For instance, I run training programs for executive, career, and business coaches. Every day at least one person calls me to tell me that they would love to coach executives, but they worry that they won't succeed. These are just a few of their reasons:

- I am too young, so no one will hire me.

- I am too old, so no one will hire me.

- I don't have an MBA, so no one will hire me.

- I have an MBA, so I am too generic.

- I don't have the right experience.

- I am a woman and don't think male executives will want to open up to me.

- I am a man and think female coaches have an easier time gaining trust.

- I have never been my own boss before.

- I don't have enough money.

- I don't have enough time to be successful at this.

- I get distracted too easily.

- I'm not established.

- I know a coach who isn't doing so well, and I don't think I can do any better than he does.

- I know a coach who makes almost a million dollars a year doing this and I don't think I can ever succeed like he has.

- The coaching business is too mature, and so it is too late for me to break in.

- No one will hire me during the recession.

- Times are good, so the market is saturated.

- I don't know enough people to make this work.

- I do lots of coaching for free, and I doubt I can charge money for my knowledge.

- I don't know enough.

- I haven't written a book, so no one will take me seriously.

- I live in a rural area, and there are no clients here.

- I live in a city, and there is too much competition here.

- No one in my family has ever done anything like this before, so I probably won't be successful.

- I tried going solo before, and it didn't work, so it won't work this time, either.

- I'm horrible at selling myself.

As Henry Ford said, "*Whether you think you can* or *whether you think you can't, you*'re right.*" Remember the guerrilla mindsets for success. You create your own inner state. You can choose to believe whatever you want. If you have certain beliefs that don't serve you or aren't accurate, you can reframe them. You are a guerrilla! You are tough, resilient, and able to choose the beliefs that support your true aspirations.

One way to reframe beliefs is by taking your perceived weaknesses and turning them into strengths. For instance, instead of thinking you won't get hired because you don't have an MBA, you could believe: "I don't have an MBA, and that's what sets me apart. I have years of practical, street-smart experience and am able to come up with innovative, entrepreneurial solutions to problems without using the tired old frameworks that everyone else learned in business school."

Similarly, instead of thinking that you live in a rural area and so can't set up a consulting practice, you could reframe that belief into one that is more supportive: "Thanks to the Internet, I can become an international expert in my niche, as long as I become visible to my target market and show them why I am credible. Also, by being in a rural area, I come across as inaccessible, like a guru on the mountaintop, and that makes me more valuable."

There is one more factor that is crucial to understand about some of our beliefs. Most people are aware of the costs of their limiting beliefs. For instance, they cause us to be afraid, they keep us from taking action, they limit our possibilities in life, or they make us come across as victims instead of as successes. However, people they rarely see the benefits they get from their limiting beliefs. We don't carry around a limiting belief for decades—one that becomes unconscious and automatic—unless we get something in return.

There are many possible benefits we might receive from a limiting belief. We stay safe and secure. We don't risk looking foolish. We remain in control. We remain invulnerable because we don't take risks. We get to say we were right all along, because we quit after the tiniest setback. We get to be above-it-all, explaining to others why nothing will work. We get to be lazy.

Let me ask you some simple questions: Would you rather be safe or successful? Would you rather look good or be successful? Would you rather be in control or be successful? Would you rather appear smart or be successful? Would you rather be invulnerable or successful? Would you rather be accepted by your parents or successful? Would you rather be right or successful? Would you rather be above-it-all or successful? Would you rather be doing what everyone else is doing or be successful?

Believe it or not, most people get more benefits by being safe, looking good, being in control, and appearing smart than they do by taking risks and completing the hard work needed to succeed. This has to be true, because, if the benefits didn't outweigh the costs, we wouldn't keep the beliefs. We wouldn't let them dictate our actions, in some cases for our whole lives.

Our limiting beliefs are insidious. They are automatic. We often don't notice them. If we let them, they cause us to sabotage our success. Sometimes the best we can do is to become aware of our limiting beliefs by noticing them when they come up, which could be every few minutes for some of us. Then we can choose to ignore them and act based on more powerful beliefs that we create. It takes time, patience, courage, and discipline to make a new and more empowering belief habitual, especially after we have been carrying around other beliefs for so long.

What are the biggest limiting beliefs you have about your career, success, getting ahead, and achieving your most ambitious and inspiring goals? How does this belief tend to determine your speech and actions? What are the costs of this belief? What benefits do you get from this belief? What would be a more powerful belief that you could use to reframe it and achieve true success?

For more information and tools to uncover and overcome limiting beliefs, visit www.bulletproofcareer.com.

CHAPTER 9

CASH IS A CAREER COMPETITIVE ADVANTAGE

ash is a wonderful thing to have during uncertain times. Cash buys you time to find the right opportunities. With cash, you gain time to relax and not panic. You can find alternatives and increase your negotiating power. You can leave situations that have become dead ends, thanks to what is often called F.U. Money. You have your own seed capital to test business ideas without involving investors.

During the recent Great Recession, many talented professionals lost their homes, and many smart entrepreneurs lost their businesses because they ran out of money. Learn a lesson from them. If something happens to you—and the way the world is today, it probably will, perhaps sooner than you expect—you need to have your financial situation in order.

First, take an honest look at the cash that really comes in and goes out of your life. You can't control what you don't measure. Start counting every penny you spend, whether with a written journal, a tool like Intuit's Quicken, or a free online financial tracking service. Otherwise, you are living in denial about your finances.

Once you see where you really spend your money, take a hard look at how much you really need to spend. Do you really need to eat lunch out three days a week? Do you need to lease a luxury automobile? Do you need to pay a pool guy to test the chemicals in your pool every week? Do your kids need to go to private school, or have the latest Wii games? Do you need to save for them to go to an Ivy League school, even at the expense of your own retirement? Do you need to own a home and pay all of the associated maintenance costs when renting might make more sense? Do you need all of those monthly wireless bills? Do you need to spend so much on clothing and trips to the mall? Do you need premium cable? Do your kids need cell phone service with unlimited text messaging?

This process is not easy. Especially in the United States, many of us believe that happiness comes from what we have. We feel entitled to a certain standard of living, and as we grow older, we expect more and more, for instance by thinking, "I'm forty-five years old and it is time for me to have a top-of-the-line bedroom set!" While most of us have no problem accepting this assertion about our culture at large, few of us are willing to make changes in our own lives. If you are married, it can be even more challenging, because your spouse may not be on the same page as you.

Once you take an honest look at your finances and make some decisions, take steps to save up a permanent reserve of at least eighteen to thirty-six months of cash on hand. Experts used to suggest three to six months, but in volatile times, you need at least eighteen to thirty-six months. The Great Recession reached the point where job-seekers took as long as thirty-one months on average to find a new job, which proves why you need to pay attention to this advice and even err on the conservative side, especially if you insist on having a job instead of working on your own. Don't touch this reserve unless you are hit by a major emergency, like a layoff or health crisis.

You can do it! If you are single, set a goal to be able to live on half to three-quarters of what you bring home. Save the rest. If you are married and both of you work, adjust your budget and lifestyle to need only one person's income to cover your expenses. That way, if one of you gets laid off, the other can cover the bills. If both of you are employed, you can save everything that one spouse makes.

During this process, avoid debt and do your best to pay down your credit card balances. Your companion Web site, www.bulletproofcareer.com, includes a set of financial calculators to help you get out of debt and start to save more. Most importantly, the guerrilla pays for every consumer purchase with cash. If you can't pay cash, you can't afford it.

Once you have your cash reserves and debt under control, you can start to save for retirement and your kids' college, along with any bucket list experiences or things that you really want. Also, make sure you have proper insurance in place for your situation, including health insurance that will cover a catastrophe, term life insurance to take care of your family if something happens to you, disability insurance in case you get injured and can't work, and long-term care insurance so that you won't have to worry about who takes care of you when you can't take care of yourself anymore.

In case all of this gets overwhelming for you, go back to the basic point of this chapter. Start saving now to have a sizeable cash reserve that you never touch. Don't repeat the mistakes others have made. Don't assume that unexpected ambushes and life's negative surprises won't happen to you. Be prepared. You will be glad you have that cash on hand when you need it!

CHAPTER 10

THE THREE STEPS TO GET INTO THE OPPORTUNITY FLOW

You embrace the guerrilla mindsets. You demonstrate impeccable character, integrity, and values. You have a dream worth fighting for. You know where you need to spike in order to be successful. You've eliminated any limiting beliefs and potentially annoying behaviors. Your personal finances are in order.

Congratulations! You have laid the foundation and are almost combat-ready. You have one more job to take on to be completely prepared. This job is so important it should be your top priority.

This number one priority is getting into the opportunity flow. All around you, people you may know and people you should know are doing deals. They are creating companies, investing money, buying and selling companies, hiring top talent, engaging consultants, and putting together teams of interim leaders. You need to know these people and the people who know them. You want them to think of you first when they have a need that fits your talents and passions. That's the opportunity flow.

Once you get into the flow, your career changes forever. People seek you out, and you don't have to chase them. You get access to all sorts of high-potential opportunities and experiences that can accelerate your career. You learn about opportunities before they are posted publicly and get the first shot at them. You discover lucrative trends at the beginning rather than at the end of their cycles. You get into high-potential ventures on the ground floor. You are a sought-after, go-to professional in your field. You become established as a key player in your area of expertise, and people pay top dollar to get you on their team.

Some types of jobs and certain industries naturally put you into the flow. In the for-profit world, management consultants, investment bankers, private equity investors, commercial lenders,hedge fund managers, and leaders at industry associations tend to be among the people in the flow. In the nonprofit world, board members at prominent organizations, executives of foundations, and leaders of nonprofit support organizations know what is going on in that sector. In government, lobbyists, fundraisers, and elected and appointed officials are among those most connected. You either want to be in these roles or build strong professional and personal relationships with the people who are.

There are three steps to getting into the opportunity flow.

STEP ONE: DEVELOP COMPELLING MESSAGES ABOUT THE VALUE YOU PROVIDE.

Every guerrilla needs three messages to communicate their value to others. The first is a one-sentence hook that describes the results you produce, and for whom. If you remember the double spike grid described earlier in this book, you are basically combining the X axis and Y axis into a sentence that instantly tells people why they should be interested in you. The more focused you can be, the more you will stand out. For instance:

- **Chief Information Officer.** I am a seasoned CIO who helps hospitals get the clinical and financial data they need to run smoothly.

- **Real Estate Agent.** I specialize in selling luxury waterfront real estate to wealthy Canadians who want to move to Sarasota, Florida.

- **Human Resources Executive.** I am an HR executive who has helped emerging technology companies recruit talent and build organizational capacity to prepare for new rounds of funding.

- **Sales Executive.** I am a seasoned sales executive who helps sales managers improve the performance of their teams, especially through on-the-street selling of consumer products.

- **Web Developer.** I build Web sites that help fitness professionals attract new clients by providing education, advice, and inspiring videos.

The second statement you need is a concise but powerful war story that tells about your most jaw-dropping result. Some career counselors call this your WOW, or Walk On Water story. For instance:

- **Chief Information Officer.** In my most recent CIO position, I oversaw the implementation of a new billing system that saved the hospital system $16 million by improving days' receivables from 110 to 72.

- **Real Estate Agent.** Even in a down market, I led the market by selling fifteen luxury units in the new condominium development on Long Boat Key in only three months, all within 10 percent of the original asking price.

- **Human Resources Executive.** I helped XYZ company recruit a new leadership team and prepared the organization for a successful investment round of $3.5 million. Now they are getting ready for their public offering.

- **Sales Executive.** At ABC Company, I helped the sales organization increase sales from $10 million to $12.5 million in one year, and this was during the recession. Our competitors experienced sales declines during this time.

- **Web Developer.** In the past year, I've built fifteen Web sites that have grown my clients' fitness practices an average of 42 percent.

The third message you need is a complete marketing message. Your marketing message includes and expands on the previously-described messages. It tells people the whole story about why they should come to you when they have a need or opportunity that fits you. Use this marketing message on your Web site, in your social networking profile, in interviews, in marketing letters, as an outline for articles you write, and in any other marketing collateral you create. A good marketing message has four parts to it:

Part One: The problem you solve, and why this problem is painful to the people experiencing it. By starting with a problem that the other person faces, you get their interest immediately. A good movie starts with some sort of problem, like a conflict between two lovers, a murder to be solved, or a fighter who is down on his luck. This problem reels the audience in and gets them involved. You need to do the same thing. For instance:

- **Chief Information Officer.** Hospitals struggle with whether to emphasize clinical or financial software and reporting. This often leads to serious conflicts among the clinical and financial leaders in the organization, and, ultimately, the patients suffer.

- **Real Estate Agent.** The current luxury condo market is brutal, especially for real estate salespeople focusing on local buyers.

- **Human Resource Executive.** Many emerging technology companies focus so much on building technology that they forget the importance of recruiting top talent and putting in place human resources policies to retain and develop them. This keeps them from growing and attracting new investors.

- **Web Developer.** Fitness professionals struggle to set themselves apart in a crowded market while staying on top of the newest fitness trends and developments.

Part Two: Your solution and the benefits you provide. This is really the very first hook you developed at the beginning of this section. This part of your marketing message compels people to take notice, because you show that you can solve a very difficult and pressing problem.

Part Three: Your unique edge that sets you apart. What is it that sets you apart from others who might be competing for similar opportunities? It could be your experience, your credentials, your proprietary methodology, the intellectual capital or technology you bring to the table, or the strength and depth of your team.

Part Four: Proof of everything you have said so far. The best marketing messages have proof. In this final part of your message, you give examples to show that you have substance behind your claims. Talk about companies you have worked for, results you have achieved, testimonials, case studies, awards, publications, interviews in the press, and anything else that clearly demonstrates that you are not just an empty suit.

Here is an example of a complete marketing message:

The current luxury condo market is brutal, especially for real estate salespeople focusing on local buyers. However, I have built a receptive market of buyers for luxury, waterfront real estate among wealthy Canadians who want to move to Sarasota, Florida. Unlike other brokers in the area, I have a large network of wealthy Canadians who want to invest in Sarasota waterfront real estate. Even in a down market, I was able to sell fifteen luxury units in the new condo development on Long Boat Key in only three months, all within 10 percent of the original asking price.

Similarly:

Hospitals struggle with whether to emphasize clinical or financial software and reporting. This often leads to serious conflicts among the clinical and financial leaders in the organization, and, ultimately, the patients suffer. I am a seasoned CIO who helps hospitals get the clinical and financial data they need to run smoothly. I am probably the only CIO who has worked with implementations of the top five clinical and financial software packages for health systems, and who has also worked with some of the largest and most complex health systems in the United States. For instance, in my most recent position as CIO at XYZ Health System, I oversaw the conversion to a new billing system that helped the hospital system save $16 million by improving days' receivables from 110 to 72. I have achieved similar results at three other health systems and have been published widely for my unique approach to integrating software systems in healthcare.

Before you move on to the next section, take some time to craft your three marketing statements. It will be difficult to get visible and grow your network if you don't have a compelling message that shows clearly how you provide value.

STEP TWO: GET VISIBLE AND EDUCATE INFLUENTIAL PEOPLE ABOUT HOW YOU CAN HELP.

Many business owners and employees aren't used to the idea of getting themselves visible in the market. However, that's what you have to do to assure that great opportunities come to you. There are many ways to get visible to the people who matter. Following are a few of the highest impact tactics.

- **Referrals**. Learn the right way to ask for and give referrals. Many professionals are clumsy when it comes to asking for referrals and miss out on making connections. The first rule in asking for referrals is: be prepared to give before you get. Always think about how you can help other people succeed. Have a connection or referral you can provide them. Or, if you don't know much about them, ask them to tell you more about their goals and how you can help them. The second rule is to educate other people about the types of referrals you seek. Tell them about the value you offer (via your marketing message) and the types of people you are looking to meet. Ask them specific questions to jog their memories. For instance, "Who do you know at your tennis club who is an executive at our local health system?" Similarly, "What about at the Chamber of Commerce? Is there anyone there who can help me become more active, especially on the Economic Development Committee?"

The third rule is to ask them whether you should contact the new person directly, or if they would prefer to make an introduction. Fourth, follow up to let your contact know how the meeting went and to thank them again for making the connection. Finally, keep in touch with this person and keep finding ways to help them succeed, for instance, by sending articles of interest or helping them find opportunities that will help them advance.

- **Mastermind Groups**. Create a mastermind group of like-minded, noncompetitive, and complementary professionals. A mastermind group is a group of people who meet every week or two to get advice, share leads for new opportunities, and support each other. You can set up a few mastermind groups, perhaps with seven people each who meet regularly for lunch, dinner, or golf. If you are an entrepreneur, you might start a business club with other entrepreneurs and investors. *The Wall Street Journal* featured an article about a group called the Wednesday 10, which started in 1957 with monthly Wednesday night meetings. The group had more than twenty members to assure that at least ten people would show up at each meeting, thus the number 10 in the name. Over time, the members of this group became leaders in their respective fields, which included investment banking, television, and publishing. Personally, I would rather be part of a live, small, face-to-face group like the Wednesday 10 than have thousands of contacts on LinkedIn or Facebook. How about you?

- **Former colleagues and classmates.** Former colleagues and classmates have been through a bonding experience with us. We share common history, experiences, and trials. This shared experience builds instant trust, but you have to nurture these relationships over time. Once you learn that your college roommate, whom you haven't called in twenty years, just raised $1 billion for a new hedge fund, it is probably too late to rekindle the relationship. Stay in close touch with your former colleagues and classmates, starting now.

- **Boards.** Get on at least one board or committee of a prominent nonprofit organization. Some independent professionals, like attorneys and accountants, get many of their clients by networking with fellow board members. Find organizations in your community that have missions that inspire you, and get involved. Many of these organizations are hungry for new, talented people to serve as board members. Once you join the board, take time to observe and get to know the other people, and then get active by contributing in any way you can.

- **Social Networking.** Create a strong profile based on your marketing message on www.linkedin.com, www.facebook.com, and any other top professional networks at the time you are reading this. Be sure that your network only includes people you know well, and people who are successful in your area of expertise. In other words, go deep rather than broad. At the same time, set up a Twitter account and send out a daily piece of wisdom or advice that will be interesting and valuable to the people you want to know.

- **Online Groups.** Start an open group for professionals in your industry or function on LinkedIn. That way, you are seen as a leader in your field. Post discussions that get people thinking in new ways about the issues they face. At the same time, post compelling advice and responses to questions on online forums and blogs related to your industry or function, so that people see you as an expert and someone willing to contribute.

- **Your Personal Web Site.** Think of yourself as a solo consultant, and create a Web site that tells people the value you provide, includes a newsletter signup, has testimonials, and has great content demonstrating your expertise and knowledge. Post articles and executive briefs about problems people in your market face and how to solve them. Record interviews with people in the industry, or of yourself giving a talk, and post them as video or audio podcasts for download. Post them on your own website, YouTube, and other free distribution sites.

- **Leadership Roles.** Get active as a leader in industry associations, chambers of commerce, and other places where influential people that matter to your career congregate. Be sure to become a leader, not just a passive member. Volunteer for committees and projects so that you can show people your talents.

- **Writing.** Write articles for publications that people in your industry or function read.

- **Interviews.** Get to know some reporters and editors in industry publications, which is easy to do once you start writing for them. Advise them that you are available for interviews and quotes as an expert. Write up a one-page document covering the topics where you are an expert and that the people in your industry or function will find interesting.

- **Research.** Conduct a short research project about top issues people in your market face, and speak about it at an industry association. You might even get your industry association to sponsor your research and form a committee to help you out. For instance, if you are an accountant, you might conduct research about how accountants are handling a new piece of tax legislation, or what they think about the latest tax software product from a leading vendor.

- **Speaking.** Ask to speak about key issues for your industry at local associations.

- **Speaker's Series.** Start a monthly speaker series that brings key speakers, perhaps including yourself, to discuss industry issues. Invite leaders and aspiring leaders in your industry to attend. They will see you as a mover and shaker in the field.

- **Newsletter.** Put out an electronic newsletter to your mailing list, focusing on key issues, solutions, and best practices.

- **E-book.** Write an e-book and offer it for sale on your Web site, on Amazon. com, and via other online book retailers. Note that you can write an ebook quickly and easily. It is not as hard as many people think! For instance, you could interview industry experts and let each interview be a chapter of your book. You can record the interviews and hire a transcriptionist to type them and an editor to rewrite them. All you have to do is write an introduction and conclusion. Alternatively, you can turn a year of newsletters or blog posts into a book.

- **Clubs.** Join social and athletic clubs where you can meet influential people. I found one of my best referral sources this way. When I joined a tennis club after moving to a new town, the local pro set up a match for me with another member. He turned out to be a successful investment banker. As he heard more about what I do, he saw the opportunity to work with me. Within six months, we worked on a deal worth hundreds of thousands of dollars to me. Rotary, golf and tennis clubs, alumni associations, and young professional associations all provide you with ways to meet other influential people. In *The Art of the Deal*, Donald Trump noted that one of his earliest and best sources of connections came from joining a prestigious social club in Manhattan. There is a club somewhere that will be fun for you and provide you with opportunities to meet great people.

- **Religious Groups.** Become active in your local church, synagogue, or mosque. Aside from the spiritual benefits, your religious tradition remains an excellent way to connect with influential people in your community.

- **Recruiters.** Maintain relationships with at least five top recruiters in your field.

- **Investors.** Get involved in your local angel investor club.

- **The Parent Network.** If you are a parent, get to know the other parents at your children's school or at activities where your kids participate like swimming, music lessons, karate, and scouts. You might be surprised who you can meet this way.

STEP THREE: BUILD AND NURTURE YOUR BULLETPROOF POWER BASE.

To have a bulletproof career, you need a bulletproof power base, also called a *sphere of influence* or, more simply, a *network*. Your final step to gaining permanent access into the opportunity flow is to build and nurture your power base. You have to do this on a regular basis until it becomes habitual. If you start and then stop, your relationships will suffer, and it can be challenging to rebuild trust and rapport.

At the same time, forget about the game *Six Degrees of Separation*, where you try to find a connection to someone else through no more than six other people. I want you to be one—or, at most, two—phone calls away from the people who make things happen in your industry, profession, function, or community. Take a moment to figure out whether you are no more than one or two calls away from any of the following types of people:

- A billionaire.

- A hundred-millionaire.

- A ten-millionaire.

- A millionaire.

- The CEOs of the largest companies in your industry.

- The president of the most important association in your function or industry.

- The most respected professors from your college or university.

- The CEO of a major bank.
- A major investor in companies.
- Three top recruiters.
- The president of the regional Chamber of Commerce.
- The governor of your state.
- The mayor of your town.
- The CEO of your local health system.
- The publisher of a top newspaper or magazine.
- A reporter or editor at a top newspaper or magazine.
- The owner of a radio station.
- The owner of a television station.
- A news anchor.
- A celebrity actor.
- A music star.
- Someone who makes his or her living doing public speaking.
- A well-known professional athlete.
- A successful agent for authors.
- The head of a speakers' bureau.
- The owners of at least five key companies that are part of your industry's supply chain.
- Five of the most prominent alumni who graduated from your high school, college, and/or graduate school.
- The partner of a successful law firm.
- A leading real estate developer.
- The dean of the nearest university.
- The five most successful people in your industry.
- The five most successful people you know who share your functional expertise.

- A board member at one or more of the most prominent nonprofit organizations in your area.

- The owners of the most visible businesses in your area.

- Up to ten respected citizens, businesspeople, and government leaders mentioned prominently this week in your newspaper.

What do you learn about the strength of your power base from this exercise?

Make it a habit to assess, build, and reach out to your power base systematically. Following is a process for analyzing your power base. You should do this at least once every three months:

First: List all the people you know who are part of your power base. Be sure to include current and former colleagues, classmates, bosses, key employees, influential contacts outside your current organization, community and industry leaders you know, friends, family, and anyone else you know who can help your career—now or over time.

Second: Assess each person in your power base by answering the following questions about them:

- What are their goals? How are you helping them achieve those goals?

- What is their value to you? How can they help you?

- Are you providing more value to them than you are getting? If not, what can you do to provide more value to them?

- What are ways you can stay in touch with them that they would find valuable? Examples include sending informative articles, introducing them to other people, letting them know about new opportunities, and inviting them to educational events of interest, and inviting them to social outings as appropriate.

- How would you rate the relationship? Use a scale of -1 to +2. A score of -1 means they find you annoying or of little value to them; 0 means they are neutral or don't really know/think about you; +1 means they are generally supportive of you; +2 means they are extremely supportive of you and go out of their ways to rave about you to others.

- How can you improve the relationship?

- When should you contact the person next? What would be the best way to reach out?

- Have you educated this person about who you are and the types of opportunities you seek? Are they looking out for you? If not, how can you make them more aware of the value you can provide and your goals?

- Is this person someone who could be part of the 20 percent of your network that provides you with 80 percent of new opportunities and contacts that you learn about? If so, how can you nurture the relationship to keep that happening or to start making it happen?

- What are immediate next steps to improve or nurture this relationship?

- When should you review the relationship again?

Third: List up to twenty people you don't know but should. Take a moment to write the names of twenty people you really need to know.

Fourth: Develop a way to meet these people and begin to form a relationship. Ideas include:

- Find someone you know who knows them and ask for an introduction.

- Find out which associations or organizations they are members of and join those.

- Call them and suggest a meeting based on mutual interests.

- Call them and ask for advice about your career or business.

- Send them a note when they appear in a news article and follow up to meet them. Tell them that you admire and respect what they are doing. Arrange to meet.

Before reaching out to these people, anticipate why they would want to know you. What do you share in common? How might you work together? How can you help this person learn about new opportunities and developments of interest to their career? How can you help them make more money, become more visible, or be more successful?

Fifth: Set up your contact management system to automatically notify you when it is time to reach out to people in your power base. Rate the people in your power base as A, B, C, or D contacts. An A-contact is someone who can provide you with significant support and opportunities. Perhaps twenty to thirty people in your network will be in this category, and they will constitute no more than 20 percent of your overall network. These are the people you want to nurture and reach out to frequently, at least every month.

B-contacts are people who provide you with some support and opportunities and could become an A over time. Keep in touch with them every other month.

C-contacts are heavy hitters you don't know well but want to reach out to and build a relationship with over time—without annoying them or being too aggressive. Take it slow with these people and nurture the relationship gradually.

D-contacts are people who are on the periphery of your power base. They are worth contacting every few months to keep the relationship going, but so far they haven't proven to be of much value to you. However, you see possibility with the relationship and don't want to let it lapse.

If you follow the above steps, your power base will grow in size and potential. The people you know will become a frequent source of new opportunities for you. Should you ever get ambushed in your business or job, influential people will be there by your side, letting you know about opportunities and helping you make a rapid transition. Similarly, if your current situation hits a wall, these people can help you find new opportunities, sometimes immediately.

Also, for those of you who might be a bit on the introverted side—like me—take comfort! You don't need a huge network of contacts to be successful. You need a moderate-sized network of the right contacts. I prefer to be close to twenty or thirty people who help each other succeed in meaningful ways and who put the time in to bring mutual value. To me, that's infinitely more effective than having a Facebook friend list of five hundred people I barely know. I even know successful professionals who rely on only a handful of well-connected supporters to send them opportunities. While this strategy is risky, these people do perfectly fine, precisely because they nurture these high-powered contacts carefully and bring them value in return.

What is one thing you can do right now to get even deeper into the opportunity flow?

PART II:

THIRTEEN PERSPECTIVES TO CONTROL THE CAREER BATTLEFIELD

CHAPTER 11

WHY THESE THIRTEEN PERSPECTIVES ARE CRUCIAL FOR CAREER SUCCESS

O ver the course of your career, you may be exposed to hundreds or even thousands of opportunities. Some are ideal, some are good enough, and some are disasters waiting to happen. Many successful people say that the best decisions they ever made were the ones to which they said no.

This part of your book provides you with thirteen perspectives to find, evaluate, and succeed in new opportunities. The perspectives of lemming and bubble radar, market researcher, investor, risk manager/oil driller, and chess master help you to target and evaluate new opportunities. The negotiator/dealmaker perspective helps you to maximize opportunities before jumping in. The perspectives of the talent scout, business developer, politician, influencer, leverage-builder, and improvisational actor help you succeed in your present role and also help you prepare for the next. Finally, the drill sergeant perspective makes sure you are doing what needs to be done to achieve your aspirations, whether you feel like it or not.

CHAPTER 12

LEMMING AND BUBBLE RADAR—

Which Apparent Opportunities Will End Soon, and Badly for Those Who Come Late?

E conomic bubbles are products of mob psychology. During bubbles, lemmings and latecomers often end up losing their jobs and risking their life savings on short-lived frenzies. Here is a history of some of the more notorious bubbles:

- **1634–1638: The Tulip Craze.** Many Dutch families lost their entire life savings by paying as much as the value of a house for a tulip bulb.

- **1720: South Sea Company.** Investors lost everything after bidding up shares in a supposedly no-risk, can't lose company focused on trade in the New World.

- **1848–1854: California Gold Rush.** A mass migration to California increased the state's population from fifteen thousand to three hundred thousand. The winners were the established companies selling prospecting equipment. The losers were most everybody else.

- **1860–1873: Railroads.** During this time, railroads made up almost half of the value of the New York Stock Exchange. A panic in 1873 bankrupted many railroads, taking their investors with them.

- **1890–1905: Bicycle Companies.** This industry dwindled from three hundred firms in the 1890s to a handful by 1905 when the car took over as the leading form of transportation.

- **1920s: Radio Companies.** For instance, RCA shares rose from $1 to a high of $573 from 1921 to 1929 before falling 95 percent.

- **1959–1962: Electronics Companies.** All sorts of companies with the phrase *tron* or, thanks to Xerox, the letter X in their names, rose up and then came crashing down.

- **1975–1980: Gold.** The price of gold rose from $100 per ounce to $850 per ounce before crashing. It took two decades before prices recovered.

- **1980–1984: Personal Computers.** Stock prices ended up falling 50 percent after a wild appreciation.

- **1985–1990: Japanese Real Estate and Stocks.** Japanese stocks quadrupled before crashing in 1990 and still hadn't recovered twenty years later.

- **1997–2000: Dot Coms.** Internet stocks lost 80 percent of their value, taking much of the market down with them.

- **2003–2007: Housing, and stocks again.** The housing bubble burst, leaving many people underwater on their homes, devastating the construction and banking industry, and leading into the Great Recession.

It is great to ride a bubble if you get in and out early. The best example of how to handle a bubble was illustrated during the final years of the twentieth century during the Y2K crisis. At this time, software programmers enjoyed terrific demand, especially programmers who could write code in older computer languages. Everyone needed them to fix the dates in old code and prepare for the change in the year from 1999 to 2000. In the case of Y2K, there was no question the gold rush would end. People knew that, after the clock struck midnight to announce the new century, they either had to already be rich from previous Y2K projects or find something else to do. Smart programmers knew this and planned their next move. You should assume that every hot trend is like Y2K and will have a hard ending. Prepare accordingly so that you are ready to get out before everyone else is rushing to the door and blocking your way.

Most bubbles don't have clear end dates like Y2K. Therefore, when a bubble strikes you are playing the greater fool game. You are trying to sell your stake to someone who is a greater fool than you at just the right time, so that you make lots of money and leave someone else holding the bag when everything comes crashing down. If you don't time your exit perfectly, or if you get too greedy, you could be the fool.

For long-term career success, seek stable demand trends instead of bubbles. Learn how to recognize when you are in a bubble so that it doesn't end badly for you. With a nod to the comedy of Jeff Foxworthy and his "You might be a redneck …" jokes, here are some indicators that you might be a lemming caught in a bubble:

One: Business school graduates are flocking for jobs in what they believe to be the next big thing. With my apologies and due respect to business schools, the fact is that newly graduated MBAs have a reputation for following the herd and picking trends and fads.

Two: A best-selling book is predicting the next big thing. It takes more than two years for a book to come out. If you find out about an opportunity from a book on the best-seller list, you are probably too late.

Three: You read about a hot new trend in a popular business newspaper or magazine. If a mainstream business reporter finds out about a trend and is convinced that it has enough momentum for a story, it is probably too late.

Four: A popular pundit proclaims that something is the next big thing. If you learn about it from a mainstream media pundit, you have probably arrived too late. Others have already gotten in on the ground floor and are waiting for you, and millions like you in the listening audience, to be the greater fool who helps them cash out.

Five: Pop scientific magazines predict a trend. If you don't believe me, look up 1950s magazines and ask yourself why we still don't travel by flying car or jet pack.

Six: Motivated idiots start to get in on a trend. One corporate recruiter I know defines motivated idiots as idealistic people with good intentions but without the education and skills to be trusted with their decisions. For instance, one could argue that there are many motivated idiots pushing environmental policies that are not realistic or helpful.

Seven: A promising technology is being hyped, but it is ahead of its time or an incomplete solution. The online ecommerce businesses from the early 2000s are examples of this point. During this time, many startups received huge venture capital investments for their online market-making sites. However, these entrepreneurs failed to understand the personal interactions and total process that procurement officers use to purchase products. Nobody wanted to log onto a site that didn't connect to their company's existing accounting, ordering, and inventory management system because that would mean they had to enter transactions twice, once on the new Web site and once in their own company's software. Most of these companies failed despite inflated valuations.

Eight: You hear someone say, "The market is experiencing a permanent change in pricing fundamentals." That's what they said about gold in the 1980s. That's what they said about Internet stocks in 1998, including Enron. That's what they said about housing in 2005. Prices are set through tried-and-true business and economic fundamentals, such as basic supply and demand and expected return on investment. The essence of a bubble is that prices rise based on emotions, not on sound business and economic principles.

Nine: Aunt Edith or Uncle Skip gives you a hot tip or tells you they've invested a sizable chunk of their money in the trend. Unless your aunt and uncle work at a premier investment bank or have the last name Buffet, ignore them.

Ten: You don't understand it. Among Warren Buffet's many lessons for the rest of us, he emphasizes that he never invests in anything he can't understand.

Eleven: The trend involves unstable, corrupt, or exotic countries and regimes. I work with an investment banker who constantly gets pitched to invest in companies with sure thing business deals in places like Saudi Arabia and Iran. These deals rarely close and he has made it a rule to discount anyone who actually thinks that one of these deals is going to happen.

Twelve: Someone you barely know, met online, read about in an advertisement, or heard speak at a free hotel seminar tells you that this is your chance to get in on the ground floor. If you don't hear about an opportunity from your trusted, vetted sources, stay away.

Thirteen: People are making a living flipping investments based on the trend. Flippers buy an asset at a low price and then quickly sell it to someone else, a greater fool, at a higher price. In hot markets, especially in real estate, flippers account for a higher and higher percentage of transactions. Watch out, because, as more and more flippers come into the market, prices artificially rise until the last great fools can't unload their assets at a profit anymore. Then the house of cards collapses.

Fourteen: You see mob psychology at work. If everyone is rushing to get into a trend the way they fight over the last hot Christmas toy on the shelves, think about shorting the market.

Fifteen: People are calling this the greatest opportunity since some other great opportunity, like Google, Microsoft, or Apple. That's like calling a pop music star the next Elvis, or calling a quarterback the next Peyton Manning. If the opportunity isn't strong enough to stand on its own with its own identity, it probably is a fad.

Sixteen: People you previously thought were idiots are getting rich. Once a trend gets to this point, start your timer. This bubble is about to burst.

CHAPTER 13

MARKET RESEARCHER–
Matching Your Talents and Passions to Demand

Y ou have heard, "Do what you love and the money will follow." This statement is true, but only if someone is willing to pay you for doing what you love. In addition to discovering what you love to do and what you are good at, you also have to confirm that there is demand for what you have to offer.

In other words, you have to have the perspective of the market researcher. If you are new in your career or starting over, you can have a lot of fun with this perspective. You get to ask yourself some great questions, and you should ask advice from your network and do independent research to answer them. For instance:

- What are the indisputable macro-shifts happening in the world and economy today? For instance, what are the key demographic trends, like the aging of our population and longer life spans, and what opportunities are they creating? What are new technologies that will take hold, and what opportunities do those create for me? Which resources are getting scarce, like water, oil, and other commodities, and how might I capitalize on that? What cultural changes are taking place, such as a shift to simple and green living?

- What are jobs that cannot be outsourced, like plumbing, electrical work, landscaping, hairstyling, producing locally grown food, and what opportunities do those create for me?

- What do Bureau of Labor Statistics suggest are the jobs with the best growth rates?

- What jobs can easily be done at a fraction of the cost by people in other countries? How can I either avoid these professions or make money by facilitating the outsourcing?

- What types of industries will experience stable demand over time, because they focus on things people always need, like food, clean water, and healthcare?

- Which new industries are emerging? Which are on the decline and will probably not recover in the next few years, like bicycles back in the early 1900s?

- What are important shifts in consumer preferences and how people buy?

- Which consumer groups are getting more buying power, like kids approaching their teenage years and nicknamed "tweens," and what opportunities are there to serve their wants and needs?

- What do I need to do to be indispensable in any of the above trends that are of most interest to me?

If you already run a company or have a stable career, you still need to consider the above questions, and also answer the following ones:

- How do I need to adapt as a result of likely changes in demand from the people who hire me or buy my products or services?

- What are emerging and growing markets for my products or services? How can I capitalize on these new markets?

- What are declining markets for my products or services? How can I make up revenues from the decline in these markets, or steal market share from others who exit before me?

- What factors could lead to a sharp drop in demand for what I offer? How will I adapt if that happens?

- What are the key opportunities in my field?

- What are the key threats from government regulation and new laws, competition, outsourcing, industry consolidation, new technologies, and substitutes for what I offer?

- What are newer companies and other professionals doing that I don't do or don't know how to do? What can I do to keep up?

- What do I need to do to stay at the top of my game, remain indispensable, and meet the needs of my most profitable or attractive customers?

- What are my key strengths compared to competitors? How can I build on these?

- What are the key weaknesses I need to correct in order to remain competitive in the market? What's my plan to tackle these weaknesses?

- What sets me apart from my competition? What do I have to offer in terms of experience, a track record, proprietary technology, a proprietary process or approach, speed and agility, knowledge, breadth and depth of abilities, strategic alliances, pricing, or anything else that truly sets me apart as unique and better? In other words, what is something that the market cares strongly about and that I do best?

Take a moment now and answer the above questions about your current situation. What is one insight you gain? What is one action you can take immediately to be more responsive to current and changing market demand?

CHAPTER 14

INVESTOR–
Is This Opportunity Solid?

The investor perspective forces you to do due diligence on a particular company or opportunity to make sure that it is solid. If you are starting a company, the perspective of the investor assures you that you are making good use of your time and money compared to other investments. If you are joining a company as an employee, this perspective will confirm that your prospective employer has a bright future so that you can grow, continue to advance, and maybe even get rich. Freelancers can use the investor perspective to consider ways to dominate their niche, grow a firm, and evaluate clients with whom they might want a long-term relationship.

You can get lots of information about publicly traded companies from the investment pages of their Web sites and from investment research Web sites. If you are assessing private companies and opportunities, ask your potential employers or business partners to give you the information you think is appropriate for you to decide if you want to work with them.

Questions that a good investor asks include:

- **How big can this opportunity get?** Investors don't waste time with opportunities that don't have a huge market or room to expand into new markets. They need reasons why an opportunity can become large and lucrative. Is the market and company growing? If you are an employee, what are the pathways for you to grow with it? Can you get rich with this opportunity? Can you create the lifestyle you want to have? Will you meet the kinds of people who can help you later on in your career?

- **How strong is the leadership team?** Investors are looking for winners, dynamos that have a track record of success and integrity. No matter how much potential a business opportunity seems to have, if you aren't working with a crack team, the potential probably won't be realized.

- **What is the revenue and profit model?** Investors want to see a clear path to profits. Does the opportunity include recurring revenues from customers or clients, for instance via a subscription, service contract, or ongoing licensing fee? Do customers continue to buy additional products and services? Is the profit margin healthy? Are fixed costs relatively low so that the company doesn't need lots of revenues every month to cover their nut?

- **What is the edge?** Investors want companies that have a clear edge over the competition. If you are joining a company as an employee, management had better be able to tell you why their company can compete and dominate the market. If you are starting a company or going solo, you need to answer this question yourself. Having good people, excellent service, and competitive prices don't count as edges. You need an edge with substance: proprietary products and technology; exclusive marketing channels; an exclusive source of supply, for instance for oil, diamond, or cement companies; size and scale that no one else can match; deep understanding of and intimacy with a particular niche market; a proven way to innovate and come up with leading products like Apple and Nike; depth and breadth of your solutions; or superior operations along the lines of Southwest Air and Wal-Mart.

- **How well can it deliver?** An edge is nothing without the ability to get results. The company needs to have a platform in place to execute. It needs the right technology, systems, processes, people, resources, and roles and responsibilities in order to get results and meet specific goals.

- **How strong is the balance sheet?** Just as you need to have strong cash reserves, you want to be sure that any company you work for or with has a strong balance sheet and cash flow. Why join a company that is on the verge of running out of cash, has too much debt to be able to afford interest and any balloon payments, and is not going to be able to pay you for your time and effort?

- **How well is it doing compared to the competition?** Check out the competitors' products, services, pricing, stock performance if applicable, analyst reports, and marketing materials to get a sense of who is winning in the market and why. At the same time, consider whether it is hard or easy for new competitors to get into the game, possibly saturating the market or causing prices to fall.

- **What power does the company have over consumers and suppliers?** Profitable companies are usually powerful companies. Wal-Mart is an example of a company with huge power over its suppliers. They can basically call the shots thanks to their huge distribution and the fragmented nature of their eighty thousand suppliers. If you live in an area with a single hospital covering the whole county, that hospital has lots of power over its market.

- **Where does it stand in the overall industry?** A strong company or opportunity offers a solution that is central to its industry. For instance, during the Gold Rush, the people who made the money were the ones offering supplies to the prospectors, not the prospectors themselves. During the dot com boom, the companies that made the most money were the suppliers of tools and platforms, like Cisco and BEA, instead of the people using their tools to build Web sites.

- **What can go wrong?** Investors shrewdly calculate the risks of bad things happening. What could cause the market to disappear? What might cause supplies to dry up? What new technology could change the industry over night? What if a key person leaves? Investors avoid situations where the risks are too large or out of their control.

At the end of his due diligence, the investor wants a compelling story that makes the hairs on the back of his neck stand up with excitement. For instance, in 1987, my college roommate did some due diligence on a new publicly traded company called Microsoft. He liked what he saw, applied for a job there, and, twenty-three years later, he was still there, in an executive role. We talk every couple of years, and while I've never asked him directly how much he is worth, I know he is really, really rich. He had the foresight and smarts to pick a winner and take it for a fantastic ride.

In contrast, in 2005 I decided to invest some of my money into a fledgling professional mixed martial arts, or MMA fighting league. I was excited by the buzz that the Ultimate Fighting Championships (UFC) was getting, and I thought they would eventually buy a local, grassroots fight league or at that I would at least be able to sell television rights. Looking back after losing $250,000 on this debacle, I realize I didn't do my due diligence like a smart investor. In hindsight, our leadership team was inexperienced, we had no control over things like whether fighters would show up or not, the competition for the entertainment dollar was fierce, we had no real edge because every local promoter used the same local fighters despite our team gimmick, and the UFC was never going to buy us out because we had nothing to offer them.

Be like my former roommate who went to Microsoft—not like me during my MMA misadventure. Think like a smart investor.

CHAPTER 15

RISK MANAGER/OIL DRILLER—
How Can I Maximize Upside
and Minimize Downside?

It is easy to dream about the upside of any opportunity. It is equally important to minimize the downside. The risk manager/oil driller perspective helps you do that.

An oil driller knows that out of ten oil holes, maybe one will be a gusher. He reduces his risk by testing a new hole carefully and at low cost, looking for positive signs before investing huge dollars. If a hole looks dry, he moves on. He doesn't put everything he has into building a pump to learn whether there is oil in a hole. In any opportunity, consider your upside and compare it to your potential downside. If the upside isn't substantial compared to the time and money it can cost you, including the opportunity cost of missing out on other jobs and ventures, say no.

The risk manager also makes it a habit to assess things that can go wrong, the probability that they will go wrong, and what the impact will be on you if they do go wrong. That way, you can prioritize your risks and work to mitigate the biggest ones while preparing ahead of time in case really bad things happen. With the risk manager's perspective, you never get ambushed, because you are ready for Murphy's Law. If you are an employee, give some thought to all of the things that can jeopardize your job security, your status in the company, your relationship with your boss, your future compensation, and your overall career trajectory there. How can you take steps to address those risks now?

I got my first exposure to brilliant risk management immediately after graduating from business school, although I was still too green to realize it at the time. I was working for one of the best-run, most profitable private companies in the world. The founder of the company had developed a process to test new products for less than $10,000 and only roll out the products that could make hundreds of thousands of dollars or more. He tested each new product carefully, with an advertisement in a regional newspaper and a small mailing to his customer list. If the product performed well, he expanded his advertising. His downside on any product was low, and he had developed a system that pretty much guaranteed that three out of every ten products would be modestly profitable, while one out of every ten products earned huge returns.

Compare this company owner's risk management skills to the way I handled the MMA fight league, discussed in the previous chapter. The economics of a locally promoted fight are difficult, especially in a heavily regulated state like Florida. It cost me $60,000 to put on a fight, plus another $15,000 in overhead to build the brand and pay for ongoing expenses. To break even, we had to fill our thirty-five hundred-seat arena to 80 percent capacity each and every time. That was just to break even! In other words, our upside only came with near sell-outs and the low possibility of selling television rights if we ever became successful. We risked $75,000 of our own money every fight to make perhaps $25,000 in profit. Our second fight, we tried a new arena in a market we didn't know and sold less than 50 percent of the seats. I lost my shirt on that event.

Fortunately, I did one thing right as a risk manager in this situation: I promised myself and my wife that I would shut down the business if I lost more than a set amount of money. Once I hit my limit, I walked away from the business, and I'm glad I did. It was the one smart thing I did during this experience, and you should do the same in any job or business venture you get into. Set a limit and stick to it. It can be a monetary limit, or you can just say to yourself, "If things don't improve by this date, I am out of here, and I am going to start looking today for other alternatives while also saving my money in case I decide to just walk." If you find yourself in a dead-end job with a client that isn't profitable, or in a business that is draining you of your life savings, you need a non-negotiable limit so you get out before the suffering becomes unbearable.

I learned my lesson from the MMA failure. Now I follow the same practices I learned from that highly profitable direct marketing company where I worked after business school. I start Web sites now for less than $1,500, and roll out the ones that have the potential to earn me a hundred times that investment back. My downside is $1,500. My upside is hundreds of times that! I went from a poor risk manager to an oil driller.

Consider another example that many people evaluate poorly from a risk standpoint. Suppose you are thinking about buying a single territory from a relatively new franchise. You have to invest a good part of your life savings to buy the franchise territory. What's your downside, given that you are joining a franchise and buying into a supposedly proven system? It could be more than you think. More than a few franchisees have lost everything they owned in a supposed sure thing franchise opportunity. Aside from parting with a sizeable initial investment, they committed to paying an ongoing stream of royalties and minimum fees, they joined a franchise that hadn't really proven its business model despite its marketing hype, and then they couldn't sell their territory before running out of cash. Meanwhile, they limited their upside because they couldn't expand their business beyond their territory, and if they had been able to sell their territory, they would have received a much lower price than if they had built up their own private business. Even if they managed to eke out a living after a year or two of struggle, they resented the franchisor because they eventually figured out that they could have started a business on their own without all of those fees and royalties.

Buying a single unit franchise from a franchisor is like buying a risky job. You are going to work hard, put your faith in a company you don't know well, and never have the upside you could get starting your own company. On the other hand, becoming a master licensee of an established franchise with a proven profit model and documented results, where you control a major territory and develop or sell multiple franchise units to others, may have much more upside. At the same time, why think small? You can build a business, create repeatable systems and processes, and then turn it into a franchise. That way, you reap the full rewards of your intellectual property and systems.

A third example applies to the upside and downside when investing in education. A high school graduate in my family decided to become a nurse. She weighed two options. First, she could get a two-year associate's degree in nursing. Second, she could spend four years to get her bachelor's degree. The bachelor's degree held more prestige, and she valued a four-year over the two-year degree. However, thanks to a shortage of nurses, she found out that she could earn $70,000 per year with just the associate's degree. The bachelor's degree would take her two additional years to complete and cost thousands of additional tuition dollars along with the opportunity cost of not working. Also, the enhanced degree would increase her salary by only $20 per week. Finally, many employers in her town were willing to pay half of her tuition to complete her bachelor's degree while she worked for them. In this case, the decision was a no-brainer for her ... get the two-year degree while demand for nurses was high, earn $70,000 per year, and let the employer pay half for her to get her bachelor's degree. After that, she could go back to school for a Master's so that she could move into a management role and make enough additional salary to justify the additional investment.

In your career, you will measure upside and downside in more ways than solely by how much money you make. Criteria for you to assess include: fulfillment, fit with your core values, work experience, lifestyle, total benefits package, culture, the people you meet, travel, flexibility, responsibility, authority, variety, independence, teamwork, fun, balance, visibility, and many more. You need to know who you are and what you value in order to assess your own upside and downside in any opportunity. If you are just starting out in your career, it can take time to figure out exactly how you define upside. You might have to experience a few unpleasant situations while you find out what you value and what you don't. Once you become more seasoned and really know yourself and the environment, you can target opportunities that meet your criteria and risk profile.

CHAPTER 16

CHESS MASTER—
What's My Best Next Move?

he chess master evaluates as many potential future scenarios as possible before making a move. He constantly thinks about the best pathway to checkmate and how to handle obstacles along the way.

Consider your present situation and your long-term career aspirations. What are potential next roles, opportunities, or projects that will get you closer? Where could each of those possibilities lead you next? Think at least three or four moves out.

For instance, I know a number of physicians in the United States who worry about the government's takeover of the healthcare industry. They are each weighing their best options. One family practice physician figured out that it made no sense to continue working full-time as a doctor in a huge family practice. About halfway through his career, he felt worn out by the pace of a busy private practice. He realized that the future promised more paperwork, more regulations, and less money. He considered getting his MBA but decided the MBA degree wouldn't offer him what he needed and, given his family and financial obligations, wouldn't be feasible. Ultimately, he reached out to the lead administrator in his practice and negotiated an arrangement to be the head physician administrator half of the time while continuing to practice medicine the other half. That way, he could stay flexible while also preparing the way for a career in hospital or practice administration. That seemed like a strong next move in an uncertain time for doctors.

A second family practice physician reached a similar conclusion and made a more dramatic choice. He was so frustrated practicing medicine that he decided to stop as soon as possible. He calculated that his best next move was to make a clean break from direct patient care and get into the administrative side. He went back to school to earn an MBA, thanks in part to his wife, who was working and could provide income for the family. He used his new degree and knowledge to get a job as an executive in an insurance company.

A third family practice physician, fresh out of medical school, realized immediately that he didn't want to practice medicine. Like the other two physicians, he saw more opportunity on the business side of the industry but wanted to learn more about innovative companies in the field. He got a job at a healthcare consulting firm where he gained exposure to many different types of healthcare companies and made top-level contacts. His consulting work positioned him at the center of the opportunity flow. After a few years he was recruited to join an innovative healthcare software startup. When that firm was sold, he joined a venture capital firm focused on healthcare companies.

These physicians understood how to think like chess masters. They knew what they wanted and didn't want in their careers. They viewed a career as a series of moves on the way to fulfillment, satisfaction, and financial reward. They considered their options and took smart steps to make the best next move possible. Most importantly, they didn't just stand still, waiting for their careers to be checkmated by forces outside their control.

CHAPTER 17

NEGOTIATOR/DEALMAKER—
How Can I Gain an Edge?

egotiating is a key skill in a fluid, ever-changing career and business marketplace. It is such an important skill that, if you have never done so, you should immediately sign up for a training program in negotiating.

The key to getting what you want in any negotiation is to have an edge. You gain an edge through information about what the other party wants. You can help them win, too, when you know what you both want and what will be deal breakers. Ask for what you want to know without coming across as entitled or obnoxious, and have alternative backup plans if your negotiation efforts fall through.

Following are four principles to think like a top negotiator.

One: Decide on your bottom line. That way, you know ahead of time which terms you are and are not willing to accept. Your bottom line depends on how many alternatives you have. The negotiation researchers at the Harvard Negotiation Project call this the BATNA, or Best Alternative to a Negotiated Agreement. For instance, if lots of clients want to hire you for your consulting services, you are in a much better position to ask for the price and terms that you really want. If you don't have any clients and have to pay the rent, you have to make a decision about the lowest compensation you are willing to accept, given that your only alternative is to spend more time on business development. Never let a hint of desperation show in any negotiation; that's a sure way to lose your edge. At the same time, don't accept a sub-par deal that you will resent. That is a set up for potential liabilities and risks and will not profit you over time.

Two: Before you go into any negotiation, get as much information as you can about the other party and his goals. Look him up on Google. Talk to people who know him. Ask questions about his goals, needs, and budget. Think ahead of time about creative ways you can help him achieve his goals while you achieve yours. Test out different ideas with him, for instance by asking, "Suppose I were to do X for you in exchange for Y. Would that be of value to you?" Ask what other options he has so that you know whether you are his only choice, and ask what kinds of terms others might be offering.

Three: Always get a quid pro quo, or something for something, when the other party asks for something he wants. If he wants a better price, ask for cash up front. If he wants to pay you a lower salary, ask for a signing bonus. If he wants you to start in a month, ask for a down payment today.

Four: Prepare ahead of time in case things start to go south in a negotiation. For instance, if the other party gets emotional or presents information that is new to you, don't let the situation deteriorate. Excuse yourself. Take a break and calm down. Rethink your strategy. Then reengage. The Harvard Negotiation Project leaders call this "going to the balcony."

In my coaching and consulting business, I constantly negotiate with prospects. Consultants sometimes waste their time on prospects who will never become clients but who want to pick the consultant's brain and get advice for free. I've learned how to stay on equal ground with these prospects and quickly figure out who is wasting my time and who isn't. For instance, I don't pursue any opportunity unless I've confirmed that a prospect has a true problem and the budget and timeline to solve it. If he tells me he doesn't have enough money to pay me, I politely ask him if he would like to start with a smaller project instead. If he still doesn't have enough money, I thank the prospective client for his time, and I move on. If a potential client wants me to give him my advice before we start, I firmly but respectfully tell him that my advice is valuable and not something I give for free; however, if he would like to hire me now, I can give him my advice immediately. If the prospective client wants to talk to other clients as references, I make it clear that he can, but only as a last step once he is sure he wants to hire me. If he asks me for a proposal, I tell him that I only write proposals after we agree on the terms of the deal and only as a confirmation that he will hire me on the terms we've already discussed. In other words, the proposal comes after the prospect agrees to hire me. It isn't something he can just think about and then maybe get back to me later.

The more willing I am to stand my ground, the more deals I close. Prospects respect me more because I am willing to ask for what I want, give only if I get something in return, and walk away if my needs are not met. People want to work with people they respect, people with a spine, not people who come across as desperate and weak. You can keep your edge without being obnoxious or dismissive, and it pays off.

Whether you are a consultant, employee, or business owner, the perspective of the negotiator/dealmaker constantly reminds you to keep your edge and get the best possible terms for yourself.

CHAPTER 18

TALENT SCOUT–
Who Can Help Me Win?

D o you remember those awful gym classes we had to endure in elementary school? Some kids always got picked first on teams, and some kids always got picked last. Whether that experience was traumatic or positive for you, think of your career as one big gym class. Build relationships with the kids who get picked first. Keep retooling your skills and building relationships, so that you always get picked first, too. If you are new in your career, look for the bosses who can mentor you. Go out of your way to help them save time, look good, and achieve more. When they leave their current position for something new and potentially more lucrative, they might take you with them.

At the same time, build relationships with peers and up-and-comers you admire. These are the go-getters who will move up or move on to better opportunities outside the current organization. They might take you with them, too. Right after college, I worked for a small Wall Street investment house that recruited people who were passionate about stock market investing. Some of my peers went on to manage billion dollar mutual funds and hedge funds. When they did, they recruited their most talented colleagues from that first job to join them. Unfortunately, I couldn't pick a winning stock to save my life, and still can't, and so I didn't get any offers.

Constantly ask yourself: Whom do I want on my team throughout my career? Build a network of people with broad and deep skills in areas that relate to your career aspirations and goals. Keep in touch with these people. Help them succeed. Build alliances with them. Show them what you can do for them, so they want you on their team, too.

Many CEOs will tell you that recruiting, developing, and retaining top talent is their top priority. As the CEO of your own career, make it your top priority, too. Be a perceptive talent scout.

CHAPTER 19

BUSINESS DEVELOPER–
How Can I Build a Long-Term
Relationship Based on Trust and Value?

I n fast-moving times, everyone is a business developer. Consider that there are no jobs or employers anymore, just engagements and clients. If you are an employee, you have one client. If you are a freelancer, you have many. If you run a business, you could have thousands—including investors, customers, and your top employees. Regardless, you need to excel at building long-term relationships the way that the business developer does. He constantly strengthens relationships with the people in his network by demonstrating credibility and value, and by building trust.

In a moment, you are going to read about relationships in terms that are a bit mercenary, perhaps even manipulative. Please don't take this the wrong way. The best business developers genuinely care about other people, are authentic, and want to build trusting relationships. They want to help others win so that they win, too. The more authentic you are, the more success you will have developing strong bonds with others.

With that caveat, business developers see their world, consciously or not, as an investment portfolio of relationships. Each relationship presents a series of opportunities over a lifetime. In this context, the people in your own portfolio can hire you or buy your products, refer business your way, introduce you to new contacts, bring you investment deals for your potential involvement, let you know about new developments and news in areas that matter to you, invest in you or lend money to you, give you advice and support, help you if you get into trouble, be a friend, and do many other things for you that provide value. You can do the same for them.

It is up to the business developer to stay at the forefront of the other person's mind, so that the business developer gets priority access to new opportunities, contacts, and information. The business developer invests in a relationship because he knows that at some point the effort will pay off. If a relationship isn't fruitful, he lets it lapse, the way that an investor might gradually sell his interest in a company. That way, he continues to strengthen his overall portfolio.

Choose one relationship in your professional life that is important to you. How well are you providing value to that person? How well have you shown that you are credible, knowledgeable, and someone with something to offer? What do you bring to the table that he cares about? How are you helping this individual to achieve his professional and personal goals? How well do you know the other person and what makes him or her tick? What are things you can start doing to help this person be more successful that, for whatever reason, you haven't done up until now? How would the other person estimate the dollar value of a relationship with you? How can you increase that value, assuming it is worth it to you?

At the same time, why is this person valuable to you? What can he do to help you achieve your goals? How would you quantify the value of the relationship to you, assuming this person becomes one of your top fans? What kinds of opportunities can he or she bring your way and over what time frame? For instance, could he refer you one client a month? Could he, every couple of years, introduce you to a new investment venture? Could he help you get a new job in a particular company whenever you need it? Set some goals about what you hope the relationship will achieve for both of you.

If you had to summarize the value you bring to each other in a five-sentence mutual value proposition, what would you write? For instance:

"Jim has a wealth of contacts in the financial arena who can help me evaluate business opportunities and invest as much as $50,000 each in a new venture, perhaps raising $500,000 total if I ever need it. He also brings me the opportunity to work with him to build emerging ventures in exchange for cash and equity. In exchange, I can offer him my strong executive capabilities in marketing and building organizational capacity to help him grow the companies in which he invests. I can also provide him with an extra set of eyes to do due diligence, while supporting him with marketing collateral to describe investment opportunities to his network. Finally, he values my credentials, which add credibility to his team when he reaches out to investors."

Once you determine the potential value of the relationship, you can develop a plan to nurture it, stay in touch, and help the other person succeed. In some cases, it makes sense to sit down with the other person and set mutual goals for helping each other get ahead. Regardless, the business developer makes a habit of the entire process described in this chapter, at least for the key relationships in his portfolio.

It might seem harsh, cold, and even Machiavellian to think of business relationships in analytical terms like mutual value and investment portfolio. That's understandable. Remember that the most successful business developers genuinely want to build trusting, authentic relationships. They seek out relationships with people they like and with whom they share common values. They work hard to know what makes other people tick and what they want to be and do in life. They have emotional intelligence and use it to know how to build solid relationships. You can't be a good business developer if you don't care about people or helping them succeed.

At the same time, if you refuse to think about your professional relationships in these terms, I guarantee someone else will. Like it or not, they are going to be the ones who enjoy the strongest network and a first look at lucrative opportunities.

CHAPTER 20

POLITICIAN—
How Do I Gain More Power?

I f you were a fan of HBO's *The Sopranos*, you saw a fascinating study in power dynamics. For instance, while Tony Soprano's Uncle Junior seemingly held formal power over the family, in reality he was little more than a figurehead. Meanwhile, Tony's sister Janice constantly formed romantic relationships with some of Tony's captains, giving her enough power to cause lots of frustration for Tony. Similarly, while Tony's nephew Christopher was the newest and most junior captain, over a short time he commanded more power than the other captains, thanks to Tony's affection for him. You could take a look at every single character on that show and quickly discover who had real power—whether a wife, mistress, restaurant owner, or psychiatrist—and who didn't have real power, regardless of his or her formal position in the mob hierarchy.

Your own organization and network works the same way as the Sopranos, although I assume it is less bloody and dramatic. Some people have more informal power than others, regardless of what their formal titles might be. A person with a fancy title could have almost no power, such as the Japanese executive pushed to an office where he is expected to look out the window for the remainder of his career. Someone with a seemingly insignificant title, like the executive assistant to the CEO, sometimes has tremendous power.

By taking the perspective of the politician, you understand how things really work in an organization. You can use this knowledge to gain more power yourself, without getting knocked off like a Soprano capo. If you run your own business, you can work to become more powerful in your industry, supply chain, and community while becoming part of alliances that can move your business ahead of the competition. If you are a freelancer, you can form relationships and alliances with the most influential referral sources, the people who can get you the best gigs. If you are an employee, you can figure out who has real versus titular power; who is moving up, and who is on his way out; who makes which decisions; which political landmines you should avoid; which projects are the most visible and respected; and who you want on your side.

Take a moment to map out the power structure in your organization or industry. Start by drawing the traditional organization chart.

Second, consider the true power of each person in the chart. Who really decides what will happen? Who doesn't decide what will happen, but has to get it done? Who watches while all the action is taking place? Who does the doing and who gets done to? Who has a big title but seems to be resting on his past achievements? Who preserves the culture and history of the organization? Who talks a big game but doesn't seem to command any respect? Who are the up-and-comers who have the ear of the people above them? If a person has more power than his title would indicate, make his box bigger. If he has less, make his box smaller. For instance, the vice presidents of Human Resources and of Sales might both report to the CEO, but in most organizations the VP of Sales has more power and influence.

Third, draw lines of influence that connect the people who to have strong relationships with one another, pass information back and forth, and tend to make decisions together. If the summer intern happens to be the chief operating officer's son, you can guess that there is an interesting line of influence there. If you know that the chief financial officer and director of marketing have drinks after work on Fridays, you can see a line of influence there. These connections tell you how things really get done in your organization.

Fourth, take advantage of the insights you gain from this exercise. Who in your organization do you want to get to know and help succeed? Who would be the best mentor? Who can help you move up? Whom do you not want to disappoint or annoy? Which issues and projects should you take on, and which should you avoid? What else do you notice?

With each different issue or situation an organization faces, the power dynamics can change. For instance, suppose you want to recommend that your company adopt a new enterprise software program. You are going to need different people on your side than you would if you were proposing a new benefits plan for the company. By drawing a new organizational chart that shows power in relation to a specific decision, you can see who gives the final yes or no, who has input, who makes recommendations, who can influence others, who has a big title but no say on this particular decision, and who has the veto power to stop the idea but can't decide whether or not it gets approved. That way you can figure out the overall politics of your idea and come up with a strategy to gain enough support.

These strategies are exactly what our elected officials do to get new legislation passed, to woo the people in their districts with power and money, to get on the best committees, and to ultimately stay in power. It is also what sales teams do to understand the true decision-makers and sell a complex project to a large company. The politician's is a crucial perspective that, once you understand it, can help you in almost any role.

CHAPTER 21

INFLUENCER—
What's In It for Them That
Gets Me What I Want, Too?

The ability to influence other people gives you the power to change how others think, feel, speak, and act. A mentor of mine taught, "In any situation you are either influencing, being influenced, or being irrelevant."

The first step in influencing others is seeing the possibility of influence. Once I was preparing for a three-day seminar when two custodial workers came into the conference room and started complaining. "My back sure hurts," one of them said.

"Mine is killing me," the other replied.

"I sure wish they'd move a trash dumpster near to this building so we wouldn't have to carry all of these trash bags across the parking lot."

"Yep. It's killing my back."

On and on they went, complaining about their backs and wishing the dumpster was in a different location. The next day, they came in again and repeated the exact dialogue. On day three, I overheard them listing the same complaints. It is now ten years later, and I am sure that if their backs haven't gone out yet, they are still complaining!

These individuals didn't see the possibility of influencing someone to move that dumpster to a place that was healthier for them. Many of us are the same way. We love to complain, but we won't or don't know how to influence others to make things better for us. Sometimes we prefer complaining and being victims to improving our situation. True effectiveness starts with seeing the possibility for influencing others to make change.

Once you know that you want to influence someone, there are five steps to succeeding. With the influence perspective in mind, you are always working your way through these steps.

One: Set a specific goal that defines precisely how you want to influence them. If you don't set a goal, you won't be able to develop a plan to get what you want. What do you want the other person to do differently? You can't just set a vague goal, like having the other person work harder, improve his attitude, or take an interest in your career. You have to choose more specific goals. Specific goals include influencing the other person to start staying at work until 6:00 PM every day, stop making negative comments during team meetings, or sit down with you to create a career development plan and agree to review it with you every quarter.

Two: Come up with hooks to influence the other person and achieve your goal. As you already know, people do things for their own personal reasons, not for yours. You need to come up with ways to get them what they want, so they are willing to give you what you want. What can you offer them that will get their attention? For example:

- Give them facts that will matter to them, such as, "If you don't start staying until 6:00 PM, your boss is going to think you are not committed to the job and won't give you a bonus."

- Offer them things that they want. For instance, "If you start staying until 6:00 PM, I will think about putting you on that project you wanted to be on."

- Tell them you will do things they won't want. For example, "If you keep going home early, I'm not going to make excuses for you anymore."

- Paint a compelling picture of the future that will get them excited: "Imagine that you start staying until 6:00 PM. Within a month, your reputation around here is totally changed. You're known as a key member of the team. You start getting to know the executive team, who also stay until 6:00 PM and then go out for dinner. Within six months, you get that promotion. Within a year, you've got a 50 percent increase in salary …"

- Talk about the values and experiences you both share. For instance, "We both want to be winners in this place. We both value hard work …"

- Call in some of the political chips you have earned during your relationship, as in, "Please, just do it for me …"

- Finally, if you don't know what the hook is, ask for the other person's advice. For instance, "I'm stuck, and I need your help. I'm trying to figure out how to get you to stay later, and I can't. What will it take?"

Three: Develop an overall strategy to achieve your goal. Based on this situation and what makes the other person tick, what is the best strategy to use? How will you open the conversation? Which hooks will you use and not use? What objections might the other person raise, and how will you handle those? What will you do if the conversation gets heated or you get stuck?

Four: Rehearse. For the highest-stakes influence conversations, rehearsing in your mind is not sufficient. Find a colleague to play the role of the other person and practice. Have the colleague throw you all sorts of curve balls, so you can be prepared. You might even videotape the rehearsal so that you can observe and improve your body language and facial expressions.

Five: After you have the conversation, debrief. If you achieved your goal, congratulations! Learn from what worked. If you didn't, don't beat yourself up. Choose whether to move on to other battles, or whether to learn from what happened and try a different strategy. Sometimes the best strategy is to apply gentle force over a long period of time so that the other person eventually hears you and comes around to your point of view.

Career success depends on enrolling other people to support your personal, professional, and organizational agenda. The perspective of the influencer keeps you focused on how to do that while helping other people get what they want, too.

CHAPTER 22

LEVERAGE BUILDER-
How Can I Achieve More with Less Effort?

everage is a term from physics that means the ability to do a lot of work with little effort. Tools like the wedge and the pulley help people get leverage in the mechanical world. In your career, leverage comes when you make more money and get more done with less effort, risk, and stress.

One advantage of building a business is that you can create tremendous leverage for yourself. Your team of leaders and managers can grow and run the business while you set direction or find other investments. Documented processes, procedures, and standards streamline the work and make sure your customers get a consistent experience. Training programs give people the knowledge and skills they need to improve performance and develop as leaders in the company. Technology saves everyone time and automates much of the work. Clear roles and responsibilities along with an organizational chart assure that you have the right positions and people in place to achieve your goals for the business. Investment capital and debt lets you build the business more quickly without using up your own cash. All of this leverage means that you make more money by growing an enterprise that is much bigger than anything you create on your own.

Consultants and freelancers can build leverage, too. First, set up referral networks and alliances that send you a stream of clients. Second, implement other marketing tactics until they become habitual and systematic, like speaking, writing, blogging, podcasting, research, getting listed online, and social networking. Third, develop products you can sell or license based on your intellectual capital. Products can include books, worksheets, assessments, how-to reports, benchmarking studies, competency tests, DVDs, subscriptions to a newsletter or research service, advisory boards, and licensing your knowledge or methodology to others. Fourth, gain leverage by hiring or contracting with other providers. That way, you can sell larger engagements to your clients or have others work directly with them while you enjoy profits from their work.

Employees don't have the same advantages of leverage as business owners and freelancers, but as you grow in your career you create more leverage for yourself. First, you can gain leverage on your time. Instead of doing everything perfectly and immediately—a sure recipe for burning out—save time by asking the key questions:

- Does it have to be done at all?

- Does it have to be done now?

- Who else can do it?

- Does it have to be done perfectly or will a good enough job suffice?

- How can I spend more time on long-term goals, instead of burning myself out on never-ending, short-term fires?

- How can I set boundaries to avoid unnecessary meetings and interruptions?

Second, create leverage by developing your people. Clone yourself! Attract talented people to your team. Train them, and give them more responsibility. That way, you can take on more challenging initiatives. In turn, you give your boss the leverage to continue to advance and take you along for the ride.

Third, suggest ways for the company to implement standard processes, systems, and technologies so that they save money while you focus on more rewarding and less routine projects. This could include getting yourself out of the office and working virtually, so you can replace your commute time with more valuable activities.

Fourth, keep improving your education and credentials so that you become more valuable to employers, investors, and the market as a whole. The more education you have, the more credibility you have, and the easier it is to get into better situations.

Finally, never, ever stop building your power base and network. No matter what your employment or self-employment status happens to be, your greatest source of leverage remains your network of people who are willing to help you.

CHAPTER 23

IMPROVISATIONAL ACTOR–
How Can I Use Creativity, Resourcefulness, and Agility to Get What I Want?

Hopefully, you have had the chance to enjoy improvisational comedy and acting at local nightclubs, the TV show *Whose Line is it Anyway?*, and various sketch comedy shows like *MadTV* and *Saturday Night Live*. Improvisation, or improv, is the ability to use creativity, agility, and resourcefulness to make good things happen. Improv is a crucial perspective to have in your career, whether you are employed or self-employed.

The most basic improvisational exercise is "Yes, and." During this exercise, you listen to whatever your partner tells you, respond with "Yes, and ...", and go from there. This exercise trains us to stop saying "No" to everything and start building on what comes our way. In an advanced form of the exercise, someone might ring a buzzer after you answer once, which means you have to come up with a different "yes, and" response, and then another, and another, until he rings a bell to signal that you are done. This kind of training builds excellent on-the-spot agility and a can-do attitude.

For instance, suppose you are looking for a job and the employer says, "Sorry, but we don't have any openings right now in the company." How could you respond using, "Yes, and...."? Perhaps:

- "Yes, and I wonder if you could use a consultant instead of an employee?"

- "Yes, and in the meantime, could I schedule an informational meeting in your fastest growing unit so I'm ready when you do have an opening?"

- "Yes, and do you happen to have an executive who would like to mentor a highly talented individual and get a fantastic intern in exchange?"

- "Yes, and I wonder if you could tell me more about other pressing issues and priorities in your company? Perhaps I can help you with those."

- "Yes, and could I request that you put me in touch with some of your suppliers? Perhaps they have a need."

Leaders at great companies are terrific at improvisation. This is true both for immediate and longer term situations. For instance, I worked with an importer that received a shipment of porcelain dolls from China. The dolls arrived soaking wet due to a flood on the cargo vessel in transit. Their hair and dresses were a mess. Meanwhile, hundreds of these dolls had to ship in time for Christmas orders; customers were anxiously expecting these heirloom items as gifts for family members. The program manager was furious at the shipping company for nearly ruining the products, but he didn't panic. Instead, he organized a party and invited his fellow program managers to the company warehouse for an emergency meeting. He provided everyone with hair dryers and combs. People worked together overnight to dry the dresses and hair and get the dolls up to shipping standards. If you were there, you would have seen MBAs from Harvard, Wharton, and Stanford dressed in business suits, acting as stylists to a bunch of porcelain dolls. They ate pizza and had a great time—and every single doll went out in great condition and on time. That's improvisation at work!

In longer term business activities like operational improvement, strategic planning, contract negotiations, and product development, improvisers look at problems creatively. They see challenges in new ways and come up with innovative solutions. They are the ones who see better ways to get results. They ask great questions that others can't or won't ask, and the answers to these questions often create new opportunities. Matched with the ability to influence others, these people not only come up with great ideas, they also influence others to adapt them.

The improvisational perspective gives you a sense of play and fun, helps you stay unflappable in turbulent times, and allows you to come up with innovative solutions that others—those stuck in the world of no—can't come up with. It also allows you to shift more easily from employee to freelancer, from entrepreneur to interim executive, from freelancer to firm-builder, from interim executive to student, and to make myriad other transitions that would be painful without that sense of play.

CHAPTER 24

DRILL SERGEANT–
How Do I Give Myself a Kick in the Pants When Required?

P eople who succeed in their careers do what needs to be done to achieve their aspirations, especially when they don't feel like it. People who don't succeed stay in front of the television, on the couch, or by the refrigerator. The drill sergeant perspective gives you the kick in the pants to do what needs to be done.

With the drill sergeant perspective, you can even create a perpetual money machine. Physicist Dr. Peter J. Delfyett, one of the most positive and motivational people I have ever met, talks about this idea in his motivational speeches. Here is how it works: Every day, go to work one hour earlier than everyone else, and stay one hour later. If you are unemployed, spend an extra hour at the beginning of the day and an extra hour at the end of the day looking for work.

After one week you will have put in ten hours more than most everyone else. After a month you will put in an extra forty hours or a full week of work for most people. After one year, you will have worked three months more than your peers. You basically add 25 percent to your productivity. It's like putting a dollar into a machine and getting a dollar plus twenty-five cents back. How much more successful than your peers do you think you will be? The drill sergeant perspective gives you the drive and will to put in that extra time and get Peter Delfyett's perpetual money machine working for you.

The drill sergeant could not care less about how you feel. He has no time for victims. He doesn't care if you had troubles in your childhood, or if things aren't going your way today. He doesn't care if you are tired or broke. He knows life isn't fair, but this fact doesn't bother him at all. If others judge you and want to hold you back based on your race, age, gender, sexual orientation, religion, or looks, the drill sergeant tells you to work twice as hard and be twice as good. He knows that you get out what you put in. It might not happen overnight, or even in a year, but eventually you will get your turn—and you had better be mentally, emotionally, and physically prepared.

The drill sergeant makes you set goals, create a plan, and stick to that plan, even if you are sleepy or don't feel well. The drill sergeant makes you get out and build your network, even if you are shy and reserved. The drill sergeant knows what you can do if you want to. He knows that 99 percent of people in the world are full of you-know-what, and he is there to keep you in the other 1 percent.

Woody Allen famously said, "Eighty percent of success is showing up." The drill sergeant makes sure you show up, keep showing up, and show up some more, until you achieve your most precious and ambitious goals.

PART III:

THE AGILE CAREER GUERRILLA

CHAPTER 25

HOW TO BE AN AGILE CAREER GUERRILLA

I f you have followed the advice offered so far, you are on the right course to create a bulletproof career for yourself. You are doing the right things to get into the opportunity flow. You have the right perspectives to evaluate and succeed in opportunities that come your way. Now it is time to take the final step and become an agile career guerrilla.

In athletics, agility is the ability to rapidly accelerate, decelerate, and change directions. Agility can make the difference between winning and losing a game, especially those that involve chaos, where an almost infinite number of scenarios can happen during play. Sports like football, tennis, soccer, volleyball, hockey, wrestling, martial arts, and basketball all require agility.

Similarly, software developers practice what they call agile development. Done properly, this means building a software program incrementally and constantly improving it. Netscape may have been the first company to do this when they released a good enough version of their pioneering Web browser, received feedback from tens of thousands of users, and then released the next version for feedback. They kept repeating this cycle of release-and-improve and, for a time, dominated the market. Agile development is a continuous work in progress, nimbly adapting and responding to user advice and changing requirements.

Likewise, huge companies also value agility. Executives need systems, processes, and people to change seamlessly with the market and ahead of the competition. Instead of acting like a giant ocean liner changing direction with a huge and slow turn radius, big companies need to dart like speedboats.

Athletics, software development, and leading large companies all relate to your own career. The agile career is a constant work in progress. You rapidly adapt to opportunities, threats, and the occasional ambush, all while pursuing your dreams and passion. You head toward your overall goals while building and adjusting as you go. The agile career guerrilla is not attached to traditional definitions of status, including the concept of having a job. Many people still think having a job is the best way to be secure, save for retirement, enjoy prestige, and move up in life. With some jobs this may be true, and there are times when it is ideal to have a job. However, I know many people who haven't had a formal job for years, who have more time, make more money, and enjoy their work one thousand times more than most people with a job. I am one of them. I had two jobs after college and then three jobs after business school. Since then, I've worked at home as an entrepreneur, consultant, author, and publisher. My wife does the same. We spend no more than three to five hours working every weekday. We play tennis four times a week during the day, drop off and pick up our kids every day at school, and never miss one of our kid's swim, tennis, or piano practices. I couldn't care less about my formal job title, how big my office is, and whether I get a company car or not. I probably don't make as much money as my business school classmates who work on Wall Street, but my quality of life is off the chart. To me that's priceless.

The same is true for Jay. Although he did have a corporate job for twelve years after college, he has had no job since then and has earned far more money and has much more personal time than he ever did with a job. One of his first books, *Earning Money without a Job*, explained exactly how that can work. Writing that book led to his being offered a teaching position at the Extension Division of the University of California in Berkeley, and to writing *Guerrilla Marketing*. Twenty-one million copies later, the rest is history!

Give up the idea that you need to have a traditional job. You don't. Think instead about the many ways you can provide value to others while getting the most value in return. There are many different ways to do that. As you read at the beginning of this book, you might shift from employee to freelancer, freelancer to entrepreneur, entrepreneur back to employee, freelancer to interim executive, and employee to student. If appropriate for your goals, you might change your function, industry, sector, state, and country—perhaps more than once.

In other words, be prepared to flip the switch and rapidly create new ways to earn income and advance your career. This part of the book shows you how to do that. It considers a number of flip-the-switch backup and attack plans that you should be ready to roll out—either because you want to or, if you are ambushed, because you must. You can launch a low-risk and potentially high-return business overnight, quickly reinvent yourself for a completely different role, go back to school without leaving your current job or business, switch industries and functions to respond to new trends or interests, find work or business opportunities overseas, and take time off to rethink who you are and what you want to do for the rest of your life.

Many people won't have the courage, persistence, work ethic, intelligence, or tenacity to be agile career guerrillas. They are like cows waiting to be slaughtered. Some of them know it and still aren't doing anything about it except hoping, rationalizing, and living in fear. That's no way to be. In contrast, those of you who have the guerrilla spirit are going to enjoy a life filled with fun and adventure. You are more likely to achieve your dreams and create the future you want.

If you are ready to be more agile in your career, read the chapters that follow and choose a few ideas to test and explore. Start now, keep your risk low and, like the agile software developer, keep building as you go. Remember that every day of inaction is another day that you remain vulnerable to forces outside your control.

CHAPTER 26

WHEN TO MAKE A CHANGE
AND WHEN NOT TO

D on't confuse career agility with flakiness. Career agility means that you can shift nimbly from one opportunity to another, when the time is appropriate. Don't flee your current situation merely because the going gets tough. Don't flit from one job to another so that you appear superficial and unreliable. Instead, make the best of wherever you are, earning credibility by achieving results, developing skills that others value, and building strong professional relationships that you will nurture throughout your career. Despite the odds, you might end up staying in a single company for many years, enjoying long-term career fulfillment and advancement.

There are three times to make a change. The first is when you have no choice. You get laid off or fired. If this happens to you, hopefully you saw the writing on the wall ahead of time and are prepared. You have a strong network of people who keep you in the opportunity flow. You can communicate your value so that you beat out others competing for the same opportunities. You have financial reserves that allow you to be patient and thoughtful. Finally, as this part of the book will describe soon, you have backup plans in place and ready to be launched.

The second time to make a change is when you find a significantly better alternative. Every opportunity is like a balance sheet with assets and liabilities, or pros and cons if you don't care much for accounting lingo. No opportunity is perfect. There are always assets and liabilities. If you are lucky enough to be in a situation where the assets outweigh the liabilities, then stay. Move on only when you find a new opportunity with an unquestionably stronger balance sheet.

Third, if you reach a place where the liabilities to you and your career exceed the assets, or you notice that liabilities are starting to add up at an accelerated pace, prepare to make a move. When you find a better situation, take it. Put another way: Don't make a transition to run away from something. Instead, make a transition to head toward something.

You have to know yourself in order to compile your balance sheet and decide if it is time to move on. How well does the opportunity match your principles and values? How well is it helping you achieve your most inspirational career goals and dreams? How does the opportunity help you meet your priorities in life, today and in the future? Do you live in a place you like? Do you have the personal balance you want? Do you like the people with whom you work? Do you have the lifestyle you want? Are you making money to save for the future? Are you growing and learning as much as you want? What else matters to you, and are you getting those things?

The thirteen guerrilla career perspectives can also help you decide whether it is time to make a change. Answer the following questions and use your answers as data to decide whether a situation has more assets or liabilities:

- **Lemming and Bubble Radar.** Are there signs that you are part of a bubble about to burst? Are you acting on emotion and impulse without also getting all of the facts?

- **Market Researcher.** How much growth and demand is there in this opportunity?

- **Investor.** Are you hoping that the grass is greener on the other side, but you haven't done enough thorough due diligence to confirm whether your hopes are real?

- **Risk Manager/Oil Driller.** What is the potential upside of the situation? What are the potential costs? What risks could burn you, and can you avoid these risks?

- **Chess Master.** What career moves and possibilities does the situation open up for you? Is the situation helping you achieve your overall career goals?

- **Negotiator/Dealmaker.** What options do you have to negotiate a stronger package of benefits and make your current situation more positive? If you have more than one career option, how can you play one against the other to negotiate stronger terms?

- **Talent Scout.** Are you meeting the people you want on your long-term team?

- **Business Developer.** Is your current situation connecting you to people you want to have in your investment portfolio of relationships?

- **Politician.** How can you better understand the political landscape and use it to your advantage? What are ways to gain more power? Can you become part of the inner circle, or will you forever be on the outside, watching as the important decisions get made?

- **Influencer.** How can you use influence skills to fix the things you don't like in your current situation and build on the things you do like?

- **Leverage Builder.** What are opportunities to do more of the things that matter with less effort and hassle?

- **Improvisational Actor.** How can you use creativity, spontaneity, and improvisation to make your current situation better?

- **Drill Sergeant.** Are you doing the tough work required to work through your current conflicts and challenges?

Two words of caution: First, in almost every workplace, someone becomes known as "the complainer." He or she constantly whines and moans about how bad things are here and how much better they are somewhere else. Then this person leaves or gets fired and is miserable. Guess what happens next. He wishes he had never left the workplace, because things aren't any better in the new situation. Don't be that person. As my mother—and maybe every mother—says, "You take yourself with you." Make a career change only when you can make a clear case for change, and when you are heading toward something that, based on sound due diligence and introspection, is better for you.

Second, don't obsess over what you should do next, exhausting yourself and those around you while you seek that mythical, absolutely perfect opportunity. If you are fortunate enough to find a career that uses your talents, pays a satisfactory income, and requires that you do work that you enjoy, you are doing better than most. Give thanks and enjoy.

When multiple opportunities come to you, be especially thankful. Do your best to weed out the bad opportunities from the good ones. Evaluate each remaining opportunity some more and choose one without regret or remorse. You will never have the perfect information you need to predict the optimal choice among good choices. Be content that you have more opportunities than most. Then dive in, make great things happen, and don't look back.

CHAPTER 27

WHY BUSINESS OWNERS NEED TO HAVE CAREER BACKUP PLANS, TOO

B usiness owners, beware! Employees aren't the only ones who need to have backup plans. The economy moves too quickly to ignore this advice. Your market could implode, and your business could completely dry up, as happened to many in the real estate industry during the housing bust of 2008. You could run out of cash, for instance, if your venture capital syndicate dissolves, you hit your credit card limits, or friends and family are tapped-out. A key person could leave the business, putting the entire company at risk. A new technology, a startup company with a smarter business model, or a lower-cost, overseas competitor could threaten your ability to compete profitably. A frivolous lawsuit could wipe you out.

If anything, entrepreneurs have an added burden, because they need to prepare two types of backup plans. First, they need a plan to prepare for the most probable risks that could hurt their business. For instance, the owner of a successful home-building company in my town survived the Great Recession thanks to his planning. When the housing crunch hit, revenues of just about every homebuilder in the area dropped almost overnight from millions of dollars per year to nothing. Fortunately, this particular business owner had the foresight to launch, or buy into, or start a number of related firms in order to diversify. He is naturally optimistic and didn't predict a market shock on the scale that we actually experienced. However, he knew that construction moves in cycles, with sometimes brutal declines. For this reason, he diversified by launching or buying interests in water removal, mold remediation, flooring, pest control, and roofing companies.

Once the housing bust happened, he shifted direction almost overnight. He moved away from new home construction and into renovations, realizing that more and more homeowners were going to remodel because they couldn't sell their homes or get financing for new ones. With his diverse interests in a variety of renovation-related firms, he could offer one-stop shopping to customers and control the quality and service throughout the process. Second, he cut his overhead to the bone and managed the administrative details of the business on his own, while also working directly with customers. That way, he easily outbid competitors who were in denial about what was happening in the market and so didn't cut costs. Third, the contractor went out of his way to delight customers, which resulted in fantastic word-of-mouth business for him. When his customers' friends or relatives saw the renovations, they were so impressed with the rave reviews about pricing and service that they often said, "Hey! Maybe we should renovate, too. Let me have this company's number." His business is thriving, even in the epicenter of the mortgage and housing crisis on the Gulf Coast of Florida.

You also need a backup plan in case you sell or fold your business and have to find something new to do. A thirty-six-year-old computer whiz, whom I will call Evan, sold his company in 2002 for $32 million and thought he was done. He assumed he would be able to live like a playboy for the rest of his days. He moved to Miami and bought a yacht for $2 million, but he got tired of feeling exploited by people who seemed to like his money and his boat more than they liked him. He sold his boat for a $1 million loss and moved to Los Angeles, where he learned to be a private detective. That didn't satisfy him either, so he started taking acting lessons. He landed a small part in a successful Hollywood action movie while chasing after aspiring starlets, but that life got old, too. He moved back to his hometown in New England to live on a secluded beach, but that got boring after a single summer. Now he lives in Hong Kong, still acting like a playboy and continuing to spend his money.

You probably don't feel much sympathy for Evan and his millions, but the fact is that he feels lost and lonely. He only stays in touch with the people he knew before he started his company. He worries that no one else will like him for anything other than his wealth. He can't figure out what to do with the rest of his life and can't seem to stop chasing the playboy life that keeps disappointing him. In my opinion, it would help him a lot if he would take some time to consider who he is, what he loves to do, what he does well, and how he can express his talents in a way that deeply satisfies him and provides real value to others. Evan's story makes a good case; even if you expect to win the entrepreneurial lottery and cash out, you still need a plan for ongoing fulfillment after you get your windfall.

Still not convinced? Here are three more examples of entrepreneurs who didn't plan and are now struggling to get back on their feet.

One: From dying mortgage firm to a career scramble. A friend who owns a mortgage lending business is struggling to hold on by hustling for the few deals still out there. Meanwhile, he is looking for opportunities to use his sales and financial skills in a different field. Unfortunately, he didn't massage his professional network while running his business. Consequently, he is struggling to get back in touch and find new opportunities. Meanwhile, his savings are rapidly running out. He has cashed out his retirement fund, and he and his wife are starting to worry about whether they can keep their home.

Two: From dream business to bust. The owner of a premium coffee shop, bakery, and chocolate company watched her lifelong dream die when the local government changed traffic patterns near her store to accommodate a large commercial development across the street. Now her life's dream is crushed, and she is out of money. She has no idea what to do next and may have to take on menial work just to pay the bills.

Three: From franchise owner on the way to retirement to having to start all over again. After a successful career, this former executive bought a territory in a business services franchise. He invested more than $75,000 and committed to pay an ongoing monthly stream of fixed minimum royalties. Despite promises from the franchise about their proven system for attracting clients, he was not able to gain a foothold in his market and drained his life savings trying. He was sure the franchise would be his final stop until retirement, and now he has to start again. He has had to sell his home for cash, has used up the savings he put away for his kids to go to college, and his family is struggling to get by while he tries to figure out what to do next.

I can give you dozens of other examples of entrepreneurs who sold, folded, or faced severe challenges that they weren't ready to tackle. I'm sure you can, too. The message is, don't be complacent. Model yourself after the home-builder-turned-home-renovator. Prepare now. Create a backup plan for your business and for your career. Keep up with your network and stay in the opportunity flow. Know yourself and what you really love to do. When change comes at you, and it almost always does, you will be glad you are ready.

CHAPTER 28

THREE RULES FOR MAKING
A SMOOTH TRANSITION

Making a smooth transition from one situation to the next is crucial. While this chapter is short, the message is extremely important. Follow these three rules and make your transition as smooth and stress-free as possible.

Rule One: It's a small world and you will see these people again. Don't burn bridges. Don't alienate your power base. Leave with grace and elegance, even if you are enraged with your coworkers and feel betrayed and bitter.

This can be hard to do. For instance, during the dot com boom, I worked with a Fortune 500 technology company. The market for developers was so tight that, as long as someone had a pulse, he could get a new job, sometimes that same week. For this reason, it was not uncommon for employees at this company to quit for any reason, often obnoxiously. Some left flaming e-mails about the company and its leadership team to everyone on their email lists. Others left their project teams hanging, while they decided to quit on-the-spot for a better offer. One associate took the company-issued laptop computer, threw it across the room, and loudly cursed his boss while he walked to the exit.

These wildly imprudent individuals forgot how small the world is. Those who witnessed or heard about their unprofessional display will remember, especially during tougher economic times. I know if I cross paths with any of these people in my search for developers, they aren't getting any work from me.

When you leave a situation, be gracious. Thank people for the opportunity. Tell them what you learned from them and what you appreciated about them. There is always something you can learn from your colleagues, employees, and bosses. For instance, I have worked with my share of bosses who failed to meet my expectations, and the feeling may have been mutual. However, even though I didn't always like working for them, each contributed to my career development in one way or another. One boss was verbally abusive. He helped to thicken my skin in high-pressure business situations. Another was weak, a passive-aggressive conflict-avoider. He taught me that, for me to succeed, I have to deal with conflict more openly and honestly than he did. A third seemed so mindless that he inspired me to start my first business. Much of the time I worked for him, I thought, *If someone this woefully inadequate can start a successful business, I certainly can.* One week after I left his company, I went into business for myself and have never worked for another boss again. Regardless of how I really felt about these people, I focused on the positive when it was time to leave. I graciously thanked each boss for the opportunity and experience and told him or her that I hoped we could keep in touch. I'm not generally known for my tact. If I can follow this rule, you can, too.

Rule Two: Take the time you need to mentally and emotionally accept the transition. Leaving a situation where you spent the majority of your waking hours can be traumatic. It can feel like you are breaking up with a romantic partner, or even grieving for the loss of a family member or friend. To give an extreme example, professional athletes can have an extremely difficult time making a transition from sports to whatever comes next for them. They become addicted to the spotlight, being the center of attention, and getting a free VIP pass anywhere they go. Suddenly the phone stops ringing, the fans don't recognize them, the endorsement deals end, and they don't know what to do. Many former professional athletes end up bankrupt, divorced, on drugs, and in trouble with the law. It can take years for them to make the transition, and some never make it at all. I know a former athlete who played one year in the National Football League before suffering a career-ending injury. While he has a successful business today, he still won't discuss his days as a professional athlete, and he stopped playing twenty years ago.

Don't be like these professional athletes. Take time to get grounded again, especially if you have been smart enough to save up some cash reserves. Travel. Read some good books. Get back in shape. Meditate. Take an adult education course. Knock a few items off your bucket list. Get support from friends, family, and the people in your network. Don't wallow. Give yourself the gift of time to accept the change. Then move on.

William Bridges wrote a number of books on navigating transitions in life. He defines transitions as a journey progressing from an ending, to what he calls the middle, and finally to a new beginning. The middle is the period when we sometimes wish we could go back to where we were before, and we don't quite feel confident moving forward to the new beginning. Think of Moses leading his people through the desert for forty years, and you get a sense of the middle stage. Although forty years is obviously extreme, take the time you need to transition from what Bridges calls the middle to a new beginning.

Rule Three: Be prepared so you don't need too much time to get back on your feet. Never get blindsided or ambushed. Follow the Boy Scout credo and always be prepared. Keep your power base strong and growing. Educate your contacts about the opportunities you seek. Make sure your skills are sharp and your attitude is tough. Save up those cash reserves. Always have a backup plan ready to go, and be ready to flip the switch to activate that plan. If you have no idea what a backup plan might look like or what your options are, the next few chapters lay out specific alternatives for your consideration.

CHAPTER 29

THE FLIP-THE-SWITCH BUSINESS I–
Online Information Publisher

This chapter will show you how to earn an income by selling information online. Almost everyone knows something that others value. The trick is packaging it in useful form and getting the word out to people who care. In fact, it's even easier than that. You don't even have to know that much. You can find people who have the expertise and market their knowledge for a passive income stream.

I have proven this to be true, because that's how I earn a sizable portion of my income every year. I sell information on topics that I know from my own experience, like how to become an executive coach or how to build a professional coaching practice. I also sell information that I license from experts. For instance, one of my informational products teaches fitness professionals how to train families in basic self-defense. I don't know much about self-defense, but I do know a former US Marine, with a fourth-degree black belt, who does. We worked together to produce a successful self-defense training manual and a series of videos. You can follow the same strategy.

Steve Martin, who shares the same name as the famous comedian, is a tennis coach in my town who has also discovered the world of online publishing. He is a phenomenal tennis coach and instructor. However, he realizes that he needs to supplement his income and prepare in case injuries prevent him from teaching tennis. Steve happens to be passionate about growth stocks. He has built up remarkable knowledge about how to use technical and fundamental analysis to predict when to buy a stock, when to hold it, and when to sell it to profit without much risk. To capitalize on his knowledge, Steve launched his FIT Stocks Newsletter at www.fitstocks. com. He e-mails subscribers weekly with buy and sell signals for top growth stocks, along with the reasons behind his recommendations. His prose is fun to read. You can feel his passion as he compares being a successful investor to being a successful athlete. He has combined his love for tennis and his expertise in investing to build his next career.

Likewise, Barbra Sundquist is a successful executive coach who stumbled into the world of information publishing. Her business began when she posted an article on her Web site about how to write a professional biography. The article was a resource for her coaching clients. Soon she noticed that the article was receiving an increasing number of visitors. She thought, *Hmmm … if that many people want to know how to write a bio, maybe a certain percentage of them would want to buy something that helps them write a bio.* She decided to create fill-in-the-blank bio templates for various jobs. Now her Web site www.BioTemplates.com has become successful enough that she has decided to focus full time on marketing it.

People are flooded with data. But what they want is useful information. They want answers in convenient, practical, and easily accessible formats. For instance, aspiring painter/entrepreneurs don't want to spend weeks doing research to learn how to start a profitable painting business. However, they probably would find value in a single, proven, step-by-step system that reveals exactly what to do to get started and succeed. Similarly, few people want to learn how to trade stock options through the school of hard knocks. Instead, many want an expert guide to show them how to make smart trades.

You can create information products and services like these, and you can do it whether you are employed, self-employed, or unemployed. It is easy to get started and costs very little to test-market a product, and you can do it in your spare time. All it takes is the persistence to experiment with new ideas, refine them, and roll out those that are successful or have potential. If you intend to make online information publishing your primary backup plan, start now. Depending on the demand for your products, it could take time to launch enough profitable ideas and generate a sufficient income stream to replace your current income.

Warning to employees: Make sure that in this or any other business venture you use your own resources, intellectual property, and ideas. Do this on your own time and not your company's. If you signed an employment agreement, read it again and make sure you are not breaking it. If you ignore this caveat, your employer could claim ownership of successful products you create. If in doubt, consult an attorney first.

Following is a seven-step process to get started as an online information publisher. Visit www.bulletproofcareer.com for even more details about succeeding in this arena. You will find specific examples of online publishing.

One: Focus on problems that people in a specific target market face. There are four classic types of target markets: industry, title, demographic, and psychographic.

If you know an *industry* or industry segment well (e.g., hospitals, life insurance, or elementary schools), you can help people in that industry solve their top problems. For instance, I worked with a company that provided information to hospital executives who needed to improve productivity and reduce costs in their organizations. Similarly, I wrote a manual to help owners of technology companies attract clients.

Title or job function can be another fruitful area. For instance, a respected nursing executive and I created a program that gives nurses the information they needed to make the transition to nursing management. Many aspiring nurse managers and their hospitals have purchased this program, despite competition from a large and established nursing association. Along these lines, all sorts of professionals want to know how to move up and compete. You can show everyone from CEOs to administrative assistants how to be indispensable or solve a pressing problem that they face in their organizations. For an even more focused and powerful target market, combine function and industry. For instance, you could help hospital chief information officers implement a particular type of software made specifically for inpatient settings.

Choose a *demographic* target market, if you have knowledge that can help a particular segment within the population. Examples include women executives and/or entrepreneurs, members of Generation X, student athletes, retirees, and recent immigrants from India to the United States. For instance, there are products on the market to help people from different generations learn to understand generational gaps and communication styles. There's no reason you couldn't create an even better solution than what is out there now.

Finally, you can also choose a psychographic target market to focus on people with the same interests, hobbies, or values. Psychographic groups include political conservatives, Evangelical Christians, motorcycle drivers, tennis players, world travelers, Beetles fans, and chess players. I know many mixed-doubles tennis players, including my wife and me, who want to learn how to win without murdering their partner. Perhaps you can help!

The above target markets are filled with people who face challenges or can't quite seize big opportunities. They want to get ahead, make more money, look good, be admired, get rid of annoying hassles, enjoy fame, win, succeed, and remain secure. If you can identify their most frustrating problems, you can create and market information that they will value and be willing to buy.

Two: Build a list of people in your target market with an information-packed Web site and with offers that compel visitors to learn more. Many people think the primary goal of a Web site is to make a sale as soon as someone visits. That's not true, although it is fun and rewarding when that happens. The primary goal of a Web site for an information publisher is to get the contact information of as many visitors as you can. That way you can follow up with them over time to establish your value and credibility. Therefore, your Web site should be full of free, no-risk offers that compel people to give you at least their email addresses. Offer a free e-book, a five-part, e-mail mini-course, or notification of your free tele-classes. Some Web sites start with nothing more than a simple squeeze page, which makes an offer for a great free report in exchange for someone's email address. Once they enter their contact information, they can see the rest of the Web site. You can test whether a traditional home page or a squeeze page works better for you.

Make sure that you pack your Web site with free articles that your target market will value. A good web designer can set you up with a blog that lets you post articles as often as you like. Each article should give your visitors fascinating, valuable information about how to solve the problems they are encountering. Your Web site should leave them wanting a little bit more from you.

The home page of your Web site should have a headline that compels people to read more. This headline should speak the exact language of your target market, to the point that they say to themselves, "Wow! This person is reading my mind." A great headline pinpoints a key frustration your target market faces or a benefit that they seek. For instance:

- "Stop struggling to grow your office supply company."
- "Discover a proven sales methodology exclusively for top-producing, life insurance agents."

- "Learn how to ace your opponent every time with a killer serve—and never double-fault again."

- "Get the hottest fitness certification in the market today, and never worry again about attracting loyal clients who rave about you."

- "Set up your own virtual assistant business, and enjoy the freedom and respect you deserve."

If you don't feel especially skilled at writing Web site headlines or copy, go to www.elance.com and post a job for a Web site copywriter. For a few hundred dollars, you can get a top-notch copywriter who will help you write everything you need for a great Web site. These individuals can also ghostwrite your articles and free reports, so you don't have to go through that process.

Once you have your Web site ready to go, you need to attract visitors to it and build your list. Tactics that work include many activities that you should already be doing to build your power base:

- **Manual promotion.** Tell everyone you know about the Web site. Invite them to visit so they can get access to the information on it. Ask people you meet for permission to add them to your list.

- **Leadership roles.** Get active in your target market community. Join key associations or groups where your target market congregates, and take on leadership roles there. Get on boards where members of your target market volunteer. Socialize where they socialize, and start to organize events to bring people together.

- **Cross-promotion.** Promote other people's Web sites to your list or on your Web site, while they agree to promote your Web site to their lists and on their Web sites.

- **Blogs and forums.** Get active on blogs and forums where your target market goes for information. Post productive comments and offer advice to those who ask.

- **Speaking.** Speak to associations and other relevant groups where your target market meets. Every time you speak, pass out a feedback form that offers to send a free special report to audience members who give you their email address.

- **Teaching.** Teach a course at your local adult education center or community college.

- **Article-marketing.** Write articles that you post to any of the thousands of free article posting sites like www.ezinearticles.com, as well as on your Web site. Try to write one new article every week. At the bottom of your article, include a resource box that invites people to learn more by visiting your Web site.

- **Column-writing.** Write a column for a publication that your target market reads.

- **Podcasts.** Interview experts in your target market. Record the interviews and post them on your Web site. Ask the experts to let the people on their lists know about the interview.

- **Internet radio.** Set up a radio show on one of the free radio/podcasting blog sites on the Internet.

- **Social networking.** Feature your Web site on your Facebook and LinkedIn profiles, as well as on Twitter and other social networking sites du jour. Update your profile with frequent references to new content you have created.

- **Press releases.** Let media in your target market know whenever you create a new free report or article for people to read.

- **Search Engine Optimization, or SEO.** Hire an SEO firm that has a track record of success getting informational sites listed at the top of search engines.

- **Pay Per Click, or PPC.** Test Google and other PPC programs. Tweak your advertisements until you can profitably attract visitors to your site.

- **Affiliates.** Once you have products to offer, you can set up an affiliate program so that other people get commissions for recommending your Web site and helping you make sales. For instance, see www.shareasale.com. It takes time and effort to manage an affiliate network, but if you work at it, thousands of people will sell on your behalf.

- **Paid advertising and direct mail.** When your information business gets going, you can test small and then progressively larger advertisements as well as direct-mail campaigns. Your ads, postcards, or letters should simply invite people to visit your Web site and give them reasons why they should go immediately to take advantage of the great free information that is there.

Three: Follow up with the people in your database so that you continue to establish your credibility and value. People are naturally cynical and skeptical, especially about things they read online. You need to follow up with people at least five to seven times with valuable, credible information before they are willing to buy anything from you. Therefore, send out weekly newsletters that offer insightful information and education that your audience will value. Give them advice about how to solve a stressful problem. Let them know about new opportunities. Review a product or book that they will want to know about. Piggyback on a current news topic. Invite them to a free tele-class that you offer, or let them know about a speech you are giving. Send your audience back to the Web site to read your most recent blog post. Oh … and slip in a sentence or two telling them about your latest information product and where they can go to learn more.

Four: Create a product that completely solves a key problem that people in your target market face. As your list grows and people see you as an expert, some of them will be ready to take the next step. They will see enough value in your knowledge to buy a complete information product from you. It is much easier to create a highly valuable information product than most people think, especially when you use leverage. For instance, a good information product can include any of the following:

- **Interviews.** You can interview experts in your field, compile the interviews, and turn them into a book. As the editor and primary author, you can write the introduction and a conclusion summarizing the findings. Be sure to get a signed release from the experts so that you can publish the interview. An attorney can write a one-page release for you at low cost.

- **Recordings.** If you record your interviews with experts, or just record yourself giving advice or being interviewed, you can sell those as products.

- **Newsletters.** Use your newsletter to create an information product step-by-step. Programs like Constant Contact and 1shoppingcart.com make it easy to publish professional electronic newsletters. If you write one newsletter per week, you will have a solid e-book to offer within six months.

- **Collaborators.** Get some of your colleagues to write portions of your information product. In exchange for getting the exposure that comes with being part of your product, many people won't ask for a dime.

- **Series of live calls.** Invite your list to join you for a series of live discussions that you record via, for instance, www.freeconference.com or www.allfreeconference.com. Then you can package the series of calls and sell it.

- **Compilation of articles.** With a bit of editing, you can package a group of articles and newsletters as an information product.

- **Step-by-step plans.** People want step-by-step plans to get results. Take what you know and turn it into a paint-by-numbers system to solve a problem.

- **Business plans.** *Entrepreneur Magazine* offers off-the-shelf business plans for a variety of different kinds of business startups. You can do the same. Help your target market get into business. At the very least, show them how to attract new business, save costs, or attract investors.

- **Benchmarking.** Provide a service so that people in your target market can see how they are doing on important metrics compared to their colleagues. For instance, hospitals pay a lot of money to know how productive they are compared to other hospitals.

- **Collection of podcasts or videos.** Videotape yourself giving advice and package those. You can market samples on YouTube as another way to drive people to your site.

- **Spreadsheets and other tools.** People will pay money if you can set them up with tools for success. For instance, my wife and I hired a financial analyst from www.elance.com to create a series of tools to help parents get out of debt and save for retirement. These tools went further than anything offered for free online. Similarly, I offer tools to help business coaches work with their clients and improve revenues and profits.

- **Member area.** Charge people for access to a premium member area where they get more detailed information than what you offer on your Web site. You can also add forums and social networking so that your members can connect in an exclusive community.

- **Coaching calls.** Charge a few people a lot of money, or charge a lot of people a little money to attend coaching calls. I know an expert in the insurance market who gets $10,000 per person per year for an ongoing series of coaching calls to help insurance salespeople sell more. On the other hand, an expert on selling skills for small business charges only $30 for a series of six tele-classes about selling. She attracts hundreds of people in each session. Either way, record your coaching calls so you can package and sell those, too.

- **Certifications.** I create programs that certify professionals in niche fields, such as boxing fitness, kickboxing fitness, executive coaching, and business coaching. Sometimes I pay a royalty to experts, and other times I am the expert. Over time, I've qualified my program for Continuing Education Credits and received formal approval from industry-specific standards and accreditation groups. I also provide marketing manuals with each program so that my customers can attract clients and make more money. Offering a certification program allows you to charge higher prices because you are giving people a valuable credential that can help their careers.

- **Books and manuals.** You can print books and manuals via old-fashioned copy machines and three-ring binders. However, with the growth of digital printing, you can set yourself up to print as few as a single copy of a perfect-bound, softcover book. You can even get an ISBN, the publishing industry's equivalent of a barcode, for your book so that you can market your book via online book retailers and distributors. See, for instance, www.Lulu.com, which I use to print the books that I sell. Alternatively, as you build up your list into what publishers call an author platform, you can get a contract with an agent and, ultimately, a traditional publisher.

You don't have to sell the information on your site to make money, so long as you attract visitors based on the free information that you do offer. Once you have a steady stream of visitors, you can make money through advertisements and by marketing other people's products. There are two common strategies:

- **Advertisements.** Even if you don't sell anything on your site, your Web site designer can set you up to earn advertising revenue when people click ads on your site. In a later chapter you will learn about a stay-at-home mom who makes an excellent income selling ads on her Asian Cooking Web site.

- **Other people's products.** Rather than signing up affiliates, become an affiliate. Offer products on your Web site and get a commission every time someone buys.

Five: Test market and roll out successful tests. Remember the risk manager/oil driller perspective. It might take you a few tries to get a successful product or Web site going. Therefore, keep your expenses low until you have a hit. You'll know you have a hit when it costs you less to get a customer than you make on the product. For instance, suppose that on your site you sell a $67 e-book. You spend $1,000 on Google Pay Per Click to drive visitors to your site. Your investment in Google nets you twenty orders. It costs you nothing to ship the e-book, because everything is electronic and is done automatically when someone orders. In summary, you have paid $50 per order, or $1,000 divided by twenty orders, and you make $67 per order. In absolute terms, you spent $1,000 and made $1,340. You're not getting rich yet, but you have a product that is profitable. It is worth tweaking and expanding your efforts.

Many people get stuck worrying about the infrastructure required to offer online products and services. That is too bad, because it is simple to get a professional e-commerce Web site up and running. A competent Web designer can recommend the best solutions for setting up a shopping cart, processing credit cards, and fulfilling products in electronic form. See www.bulletproofcareer.com for a list of resources to get going.

Six: Keep testing products and offers, even if you are repackaging information you already market. The key to success in information publishing is persistence. Keep testing! The very first information product I developed was a disaster. Foolishly I spent almost $20,000 on graphics while writing a leadership book. As a stand-alone product, it bombed. Fortunately, it did help me establish my credibility as a consultant, so I continued to offer it to prospects and clients for free. Then one day I got the idea of repackaging the book as part of a coach-training program. Suddenly I turned a $20 book into a $3,000 coach-training program. The program became profitable, gets rave reviews from participants, and is now a fun part of what I do for a living.

Do whatever you can to solve a problem in a comprehensive, elegant, step-by-step way. Try different formats to deliver your information. Offer improved levels of support, such as a year of e-mail support. Add in some monthly coaching calls. Create a member area. Give free lifetime upgrades as you roll out new versions of your information. For instance, my initial coach-training program was basically a three-ring binder and a series of tele-classes, marketed on a five-page Web site. Then I added a marketing manual and six CDs of recorded tele-classes. Now the program includes five manuals, a member area with hundreds of hours of recorded calls, approval by the International Coach Federation, 24/7 e-mail support for two years, a live seminar, and a free coach-marketing service. People from around the world are members, and corporations invite me to train their executives to be coaches. You can achieve the same results if you keep at it.

Seven: Branch out to other target markets to limit your risk and continue to build your income. Once you feel that you have tapped into a specific target market, consider branching out into a related market. If you have gone as far as you can in providing information to realtors, think about expanding to mortgage brokers or contractors. If you serve tennis professionals, expand to golf professionals. If you market to liberal democrats, find a way to meet the information needs of moderate democrats.

Keep testing and refining, testing and refining. Eventually, you can create an information publishing mini-empire and never have to rely on anyone else again for career security.

CHAPTER 30

THE FLIP-THE-SWITCH BUSINESS II–
Consultant/Freelancer

According to the Bureau of Labor Statistics, 14.8 million people, or 12 percent of the labor force, have gone solo as freelancers or consultants as of 2009. If you know how to attract clients, going solo can provide you with freedom to make your own hours, choose your clients, and work from almost anywhere. While it may seem risky to have to eat what you kill as a contractor, the truth is that, once you get up and running, you have less risk than the average employee. That's because employees have single clients, their employers. If they lose those clients, they need to start all over again to find new ones. Freelancers and consultants have multiple clients. If one client goes away, they lose only a portion of their incomes. Plus, smart freelancers/consultants are always marketing. That way, they attract new clients on a regular basis.

Following are six steps to success as a freelancer/consultant. For more details, visit www.bulletproofcareer.com.

One: Be able to solve a problem. You won't get freelance gigs if you don't have skills, knowledge, or a methodology to solve someone's problem. Fortunately, if you have worked in almost any organization for a while, you have the skills you need to succeed as a freelancer. Companies need assistance in marketing, human resources, administrative support, leadership development, information technology solutions, sales, training, strategic planning, writing, fund-raising, accounting, security, and almost every other function for which they also hire employees. To get hired, you need the substance to deliver, bring value, and get results for your clients.

Two: Focus on a target market. It is easier and more profitable to reach people in a focused target market, especially when you develop a solution that solves specific problems that your target market faces.

While you may believe your skills and knowledge apply across-the-board, your clients would disagree. By developing solutions that speak to the specific issues a focused market faces, you can create deeper solutions, charge higher rates, and gain credibility more quickly. People in a similar target market tend to read the same things, go to the same association meetings, and know each other, so you can focus your marketing efforts to save money and time.

Therefore, instead of offering your services as a human resources generalist, become the leading expert in human resource solutions in the information technology industry. Rather than offering administrative support for executives in general, become the leading, outsourced, administrative-support solution for attorneys. Instead of marketing yourself as a sales trainer, focus on getting visible as a sales trainer for the real estate industry.

The last chapter listed the most common types of target markets: industry, function, demographic, and psychographic. As a consultant, you can also focus on a specific geographic region, although it helps to combine a geographic focus with one of the other target markets, such as marketing solutions for manufacturers in Ohio.

Three: Develop a marketing message that shows your value and attracts interest. Many freelancers fail to craft a persuasive marketing message that explains why anyone should care about them. They spend too much time talking about their biography instead of about their prospects' problems and how they can solve them.

A good marketing message starts like a good movie, with an interesting problem that draws the audience in. For instance, the star loves someone who doesn't love him back. He's a down-and-out boxer who can't catch a break. He's stuck in the jungle with a vicious alien.

Your marketing message does the same thing by describing a compelling problem that your target market faces:

- "Stop struggling to recruit top talent …"

- "Don't waste time and money on marketing campaigns that don't work."

- "Stop spending time on tedious tasks that someone with your education and skills shouldn't have to do."

Next, discuss your solution to the problem using specific language that your target market uses. To really strengthen your message, talk about your specific proprietary approach for getting consistent results, and include the benefits that your clients experience when they work with you. For instance:

- "My five-step recruiting process screens out unqualified candidates and brings in a stream of high-energy, passionate, and highly skilled talent with a proven track record of success. With this process, your company becomes a magnet for top talent in the informational technology industry."

- "My three-pronged marketing model generates a guaranteed return on investment through testing, deep analytics, and skilled targeting. You will enjoy the satisfaction of getting more customers in less time, and of being able to document the return on investment that your department brings to the company."

- "I have a proven system that helps attorneys get control of their time and focus on practicing the law, not handling mundane administrative tasks. Eliminate the hassles and headaches of your practice and focus on what you love to do."

Third, explain to your audience your unique edge and qualifications. Think about filling in the phrase "Unlike other …"

- "Unlike other recruiters, I have a fifteen-year track record working with five of the top 10 software firms in Silicon Valley."

- "What sets me apart is my track record of results and my no-risk guarantee. Your employees won't return their salaries to you in productivity if they don't get the job done. But I can guarantee to return my fees, because my proven approach to testing, and then rolling out successful tests, is fail-proof."

- "Unlike other administrative support solutions, I bring a proprietary suite of tools and processes to get control of your paperwork, scheduling, tracking hours, and invoicing. These tools are unmatched in power and simplicity."

Finally, your marketing message concludes with proof that what you have said so far is accurate. Offer testimonials, references, awards, degrees, publications, interviews in leading media, case studies, and any other facts that prove you have the competence and experience to deliver what you promise.

Four: Establish credibility in your target market by getting, and staying, visible. In the fast-food industry, they say, "If you have time to lean, you have time to clean." In the consulting and freelancing world, a restated slogan is,"If you have time to lean, you have time to get out there and attract clients." Business development sets the successful freelancer apart from the ones who struggle to make a living. After almost two decades as a consultant and coach, I've found that the professional with the best credentials and experience doesn't always make the most money. For better or for worse, the professionals who consistently market their services are typically the ones who get the best clients and earn the most.

You don't have to be a pushy salesperson or use tacky marketing gimmicks to get visible. It is much more effective to attract prospects to you by providing information and education that establishes your credibility. That way, you build your database with those who want to receive ongoing education and information about the problems that they face and that you are able to address. Over time, people will start to think of you first when they have a need. You become the go-to professional in your niche. Business follows almost automatically.

The previous chapter about information publishing outlined a number of ways for the consultant or freelancer to gain visibility. In fact, marketing information products and developing business for your consulting or freelance services go hand-in-hand. They are a perfect combination that you can do in tandem. Your consulting work will encourage people to buy your information products, and the fact that you have information products builds your credibility so that people want to hire you.

Tactics include: developing a Web site with great articles and offers in exchange for contact information, speaking, writing, generating publicity, teaching courses, getting involved in associations and other places where your target market congregates, leading tele-classes, sending out a newsletter, inviting people to get a free report, blogging, podcasting, and social networking. You should also get listed on online sites that feature experts, like www.elance.com and www.guru.com.

In my own work as a consultant, I have found that starting a research project is a proven way to get in front of opinion leaders. To conduct research, think of a topic that would be of interest to your target market, for instance hiring plans, confidence in the economy, top marketing tactics, biggest frustrations, and top risks that they see on the horizon. You don't need a PhD in statistics or research methodology. Simply call a few decision makers in your target market and ask for a few minutes of their time to interview them, in exchange for a copy of your findings. This is a terrific way to start a relationship and establish yourself as a credible source.

However, the absolute lowest-cost, easiest, and most satisfying way to get hired as a consultant or freelancer is by generating referrals from people who know and respect your work:

- **Educate and encourage your network to spread the word.** The people in your network need to know precisely whom you help and how. Use your marketing message to educate them about the kinds of referrals you seek. Tell them about the kinds of people and organizations you want as clients, and ask them directly for referrals. At the same time, ask them about how you can help them, and about the types of referrals they seek.

- **Give first, and don't keep strict score.** The best way to get a referral is by giving a referral. Be generous. When you meet with someone in your network, have a couple of referrals in your back pocket, so he knows you care about him. You might not get anything out of the relationship immediately, but things have a way of evening out over time. Of course, some people are takers and will never reciprocate; there comes a point where you don't need to keep giving if you get nothing of value in return.

- **Cross-promote.** Develop arrangements with complementary and non-competing professionals in your area to promote each other's services. You can send out letters to your respective lists, sponsor panels where you present current trends and issues to your respective prospects, and agree to tell your clients about each other when the opportunity comes up.

- **Form alliances.** Every consultant should form alliances with groups of professionals in order to give clients a range of one-stop services. For instance, business coaches should form alliances with business attorneys, commercial bankers, web designers, office supply vendors, business software vendors, accountants, venture capitalists and other investors, business insurance providers, financial planners, and benefits providers.

- **Set up Mastermind Groups.** Invite groups of five to ten colleagues to meet every week or so for breakfast or lunch to discuss issues, provide support, exchange leads, and brainstorm about how to attract clients.

Some professionals get all of their clients by setting up as many as a dozen Mastermind Groups.

- **Get skilled at having referral conversations with clients.** Once you get your first raving client, you should see a marked increase in business. About five years into my consulting practice, I could still track 50 percent of my business back to the very first client I ever had. Existing clients are usually very willing to help you succeed, especially if you have helped them succeed. After a successful engagement, ask your client to sit down with you for a few minutes to discuss other people they know who might benefit from your services. Help them think about good prospects by asking direct questions. For instance, "You are on the board of the museum. Who else is on the board who might see value in your marketing services?" Once you get a lead, determine whether your client or you should make the first contact. Make a soft sell to any referral, letting them know how you heard about them and asking if they might be interested in a short call to see if there might be a mutual fit. Then follow up with the client who made the connection and let him or her know how things went.

- **Remember that the best opportunities are right in front of you.** Your current and past clients already know you and trust you. They are much more likely to hire you than prospects who don't know you well. Even if it is more glamorous and exciting to land that new client, focus first on ways you can continue to serve your current and past clients. Keep your antennae up for problems they talk about, new initiatives in the works, and anything else that suggests they need your help to get results.

- **Let everyone know you rely on referrals.** Publicize the fact that you rely on referrals for most of your business. Put it on your business card, your Web site, your invoices, and your letterhead. Add a couple of lines in your client contract stating that the client will sit down and have a conversation about referrals with you on satisfactory completion of the work.

- **Be incredibly grateful when you get referrals.** Other people take a risk when they refer you to the people in their power base. Be sure to thank them accordingly. Send tastefully appropriate gifts to clients who provide frequent referrals. Even better, help them succeed in their business however you can.

Five: Get your first client. Your first client is the hardest. After that, everything usually gets easier. Your first client gives you confidence, testimonials, and the ability to tell new prospects about other work you are doing.

To get that first client, you need to be skilled at having conversations that lead to people hiring you. Here are steps to follow to get your first client within thirty days:

1. Perfect a thirty-second elevator speech that follows the format, "I help X get Y." X is your target market. Y is the benefit you provide. For instance, "I help attorneys save time, money, and hassles with my virtual assistant service." Or, "I help physicians market their practices and acquire all the patients they can handle."

2. Write a two- or three-page executive brief that educates people about how to solve a problem that they face. Follow the format of a strong marketing message, explaining the costs of the problem and how to solve it. Spend 95 percent of the piece giving valuable insights. Close out the piece with information about your services and how you can be reached.

3. Every day, get your executive brief out to at least ten people who are in your target market. Ask these people for advice about whether the executive brief can be improved, whether they can use your services, and whether they know anybody else who can.

4. When you find someone who is interested in hiring you, ask great questions about his problems and how he might like you to help. When you understand the situation and his problems, jump in with a suggestion about how you can add value.

5. Don't offer your services for free. You want to be on equal standing with any prospect or client, and you don't want to get into the habit of undervaluing your services. Do some research to understand the going rate for the service you provide. Remember that, as a freelancer, you need to charge enough to cover your time with clients; cover overhead like payroll taxes, phone, computer, and insurance; and cover time spent marketing. Suggest a day rate that would be satisfactory, assuming you were employed 50 percent of the time and marketing the other 50 percent of the time. For instance, if you want to make $50,000 per year, assume that there are two hundred working days in a year and charge $500 per day. Later on, you can learn about value-based pricing and make even more.

6. Be enthusiastic but not desperate. Nobody wants to hire someone who seems too desperate. Show the prospect that you want to work with him, but don't come across as needy.

7. Move the conversation toward a decision. A yes is great. A no is not great but is okay because you can move on to a yes from someone else. "Let me think about it and get back to you" is torture. Ask your client for the job. For instance, "I'd really like to work on this project with you. What about you?" Or, "What would you like to do next?" If you don't push the conversation forward, he probably won't either. Don't get stuck in the limbo world of maybe.

8. Don't give up. Keep meeting people. Stay visible. It might take time to tweak your approach until a client hires you. However, if you have something valuable to offer and stay in the action, good things usually follow.

Six: Create raving, loyal clients. A great marketer will attract clients, but a top notch professional will keep them. Many people say that they don't get into consulting or freelancing because they don't care to market themselves. I think the reality is that many people simply don't have the professionalism and competence to build up a base of highly satisfied and loyal clients. There is nowhere to hide as a consultant or freelancer. You can't blame anyone but yourself when projects go off-course or your client is unhappy.

Tips include:

•   Keep upgrading your processes and methodology so that you provide consistent, reliable service to your clients.

•   Ask yourself what it will take for you to be able to offer a 100-percent-satisfaction guarantee to your clients, and make the needed improvements to your service to be able to do just that.

•   Don't accept work from clients you don't think will provide you with referrals or who will be impossible to satisfy.

•   Manage client expectations during the sales process so that the client will not be disappointed when the assignment is completed.

•   Focus on results, not just tasks. Make sure you are meeting your client's specific business needs and providing a total solution to his problem. For instance, many software developers follow the tasks on their work plan to the letter, and still don't provide a product that justifies the investment from the client's point of view.

- At the start of a project, ask your client what would have to happen for him to think of you as the best provider he has ever hired in this area, and to become a raving fan. Then go out of your way to exceed those expectations.

- Have early- and mid-course project reviews with each client. Ask how you can improve during the remainder of the project.

- Learn from each and every client engagement. Ask for advice about how you can do a better job next time.

- Give your client frequent status updates, including updates about what you need from him to make the project more successful.

- If you miss the mark, do whatever it takes to get back on track and make amends. Research shows that clients highly value a professional who goes the extra mile to fix problems that come up during an engagement. This is true regardless of who caused the issue in the first place.

- Build a relationship with the client. Don't focus on the project alone. Get to know the client as much as is appropriate. Understand his aspirations and help him achieve his goals. If your client sees you as a person and not just a vendor, he will be much more likely to hire you again.

If you plan to go solo or want to have that option down the road, start building up your network now. Without a network, it can take a month or two to get your first client and six months to a year of persistent business development before you build up a full practice. At the same time, why not moonlight as a consultant or freelancer to prepare for a potential transition? You can do work after hours from home or on weekends.

In my own case, I was working for a company that was going down the tubes before I went solo. Seeing the writing on the wall and wanting to go out on my own, I started leading free seminars about strategic planning at a local association. Participants in these seminars asked me to lead strategic planning retreats at their company on weekends, which I gladly did. By the time my formal employer imploded, I had enough clients to replace 75 percent of my income immediately. Within three months, I was running a full practice and haven't looked back since.

Remember: If you are doing the work required to spike in relationships and in valuable skills and knowledge, then you already have a strong foundation in place to be a successful freelancer/consultant. You are getting to know potential clients as well as the people who can connect you to potential clients. If going solo appeals to you, keep doing this work, and it will not be hard to make the transition quickly. If going solo is not your first choice, at least it will remain an option until more preferable alternatives are feasible. Either way, you should be prepared to become a freelancer at any time, because you never know when you might need to do so.

CHAPTER 31

THE FLIP-THE-SWITCH BUSINESS III–
Firm-Builder

F reelancers and consultants have one major downside. If you are a solo provider, you don't have any leverage. You limit your upside to the time you have for client work. You can't sell your company because it relies too much on you. Actually, it *is* you. If you get injured or sick, your business falls apart. You might be making a fine living as a freelancer or consultant, but you are leaving money on the table.

To get to the next level, you need to build a firm. A firm allows you to take proprietary intellectual property and create something that doesn't rely on your time alone. You create an enterprise that you can sell and that can generate income for you, even if you can't work.

If you sell information products while also being a consultant or freelancer, you are already on your way to building a firm. Next, incorporate one or more of the following models in your practice to make your firm even more valuable.

Firm-Builder Model One: Build a firm with employees and/or contractors. Once you create a unique methodology and approach to get results for clients, you can hire others to duplicate that methodology on your behalf. For instance, I worked for a healthcare management consulting firm that started with four initial partners sitting around a coffee table in a Manhattan apartment building. The partners targeted hospitals and health systems, offering them ways to handle recent changes in federal reimbursement. Over time, the partners began hiring smart people out of top universities to join them and help build the firm. The partners rewarded these associates for creating consulting services focused on operational excellence, strategy, and clinical utilization. They also rewarded them for learning how to attract their own clients, develop associates to run projects that they sold, and build the firm to be bigger and stronger. With this heavy emphasis on firm development, the company grew to $80 million in revenues, three hundred fifty employees, and five offices in the United States and United Kingdom. A Fortune 500 company bought out the initial partners, heavily rewarding them for their foresight to build a firm instead of continuing to sit around that coffee table.

A second firm owner I know is at the early stages of this process. You read about him at the very beginning of this book. He started as a high school teacher. Since leaving his job, he has built a million-dollar communication training firm. Tired of all of the travel required in his job, he is now cloning himself by training five other seminar leaders that he knows and trusts. By doing this, he projects that he can build his firm to $5 million to $9 million in size, while he travels less and makes more money.

A third firm I worked for grew almost exclusively via contractors. The founder started as a solo consultant, helping start-up technology firms market their products. Seeing the limitations of being solo, he made the decision to bring other consultants into client engagements as contractors. He also wisely decided to focus on a single niche—marketing solutions for technology companies. He negotiated overall engagement terms and oversaw the client relationship while contractors did the work. In exchange, he marked up the contractor's fees to earn his profit. He struggled for a couple of years to make the transition, because he needed at least three consultants working full time to equal his income as a solo consultant. Eventually, he reached the point where he was making more money than he did working solo. Ultimately, he built up a database of four thousand solo marketing experts that he could call on anytime a client needed a specialist to help with a marketing problem. His company now employs a few core consultants who lead projects with the help of the specialists in the database, along with a team that helps him recruit and manage the contractors in his database. Instead of working with small startups, his firm now boasts some of the top technology companies in Silicon Valley as his clients.

Firm-Builder Model Two: Automate results for clients through software. This model is like having information products on steroids. For instance, the healthcare consulting firm described above used to manually benchmark a client's productivity. To do this, consultants spent weeks inputting and massaging publicly available data about healthcare systems. This work was extremely expensive, which frustrated potential clients and often kept them from hiring the firm. At the same time, the consultants found the work to be tedious and burned out quickly, causing a turnover problem in the firm. Therefore, the firm automated the benchmarking process by creating software that took the client's data, combined it with public data, and spit out a benchmarking report. Clients didn't have to pay as much, the firm still made a huge margin, and consultants could focus on more productive uses of their time, like helping clients realize the opportunities highlighted in the benchmarking report. Most importantly, clients were more likely to convert to the next phase of consulting, because they hadn't already drained their budgets on the diagnostic piece.

Similarly, the leadership communications firm builder described above is also developing an automated product. In his case, he is developing an assessment tool that gives executives objective data about their communication effectiveness. Participants get feedback from the people who know them, all of whom complete an online survey, and then results are reported on a beautiful graphic chart. The results show how the person compares to other executives and what he has to do to improve. This automated product will generate terrific passive revenue for the firm owner. It will also lead to additional work for him, because prospects will take the assessment and then want him to coach and train them to perform better.

Firm-Builder Model Three: License your intellectual capital. Once you develop information products and methodologies that get consistent results for clients, you can train others to do the same. In exchange, they will pay you a licensing fee. Many training and consulting firms use this model. For instance, let's say you have a sales training program with clients who love your content. Why not invite them to become trained as licensed trainers? They pay for the right to license your materials as well as for the process required for them to be trained and demonstrate competency. You also receive fees for each participant that they train, whether in the form of a certification fee or a fee for the materials that you provide. Imagine that you license your program to an internal trainer at just one Fortune 1000 firm. That trainer might end up training thousands of employees while you do nothing but ship the materials out, provide occasional support, and collect fees!

Firm-Builder Model Four: Gain leverage through clients. Clients can also help you generate leverage. For instance, you can start a leadership circle of non-competing professionals who meet to support one another. In exchange for a membership fee, you provide them with a conference where they meet in person, you conduct research and benchmarking studies of members on their behalf so that they automatically share best practices, and you also offer one-on-one support and coaching. The members of the group set the agenda, determine how often to meet, and vote on the priorities for research and benchmarking. One healthcare consulting firm has organized a leadership circle of one hundred of the top hospital CEOs in the United States, charging them $10,000 per year. The firm receives $1 million in revenues while having constant access to the top opinion leaders in the industry. Who do you think the members of this group call first when they have a need for consulting?

You don't have to be national in scope to take advantage of this model. For instance, Vistage has created a great business by providing a monthly forum for local CEOs of small to mid-sized companies. A local independent facilitator runs these groups, which meet monthly to exchange ideas, offer support, and listen to presentations by thought leaders in business. You can create a Vistage-style forum in your area focused on your niche.

Firm-Builder Model Five: Become an expert on experts in your field. In addition to consulting, create a service that helps the clients in your niche find experts-on-call. In other words, you can be the Monster.com or CareerBuilder.com for interim executives, consultants, and experts in a specific niche. Your clients want expertise, experts in your niche want gigs, and you can be the connector in between who gets paid for matching both parties up. You also position yourself as a connector in the niche market, which gets you first crack at opportunities and talent. For instance, see my own site www.interimrevolution.com.

CHAPTER 32

THE FLIP-THE-SWITCH BUSINESS IV–
The LFC/LBE Business

L FC/LBE stands for Low Fixed Costs/Low Barriers to Entry. Almost anyone can start a LFC/LBE business. With hustle, determination, management smarts, and leadership skills, you might even be able to grow your business to the point that it takes care of your needs for good.

By definition a LFC/LBE business doesn't cost much to start, doesn't cost much to run, and is relatively easy to launch. Many LFC/LBE business owners do not have to worry about outsourcing, because usually these businesses provide local services that must be done in person: landscaping, pool maintenance, home repairs, car washing, local newspapers, catering, babysitting, fitness training, tutoring, massage therapy, window washing, housecleaning, home companion services, local temporary staffing, wedding planning, real estate brokerage, home organizing, meeting facilitation, photography, florist, music teacher, computer repair, home decorator, house painting, etc. Others can be regional or national in scope, such as virtual assistant services and recruiting.

You can get pretty creative when setting up a LFC/LBE business. For instance, the owners of one of the best restaurants in my hometown of Sarasota are a husband and wife who don't even own or lease a full-time space. Instead, on Friday and Saturday nights they rent a local diner and convert the space to a fine French restaurant. They cover the tables in linen and good silverware, do some quick redecorating to give the diner a more elegant ambiance, and prepare a gourmet prix fixe dinner for patrons. They basically have to cover their food cost and a little rent, and the rest is profit. The husband-and-wife team has been doing this for a few years. Even during a difficult economy, loyal customers keep coming back.

A second example shows that owning a LFC/LBE business doesn't place limits on the income you can earn. This entrepreneur left a major consumer finance company when he realized he was never going to make the kind of money he needed to live the life he wanted and afford to send his kids to school. He recruited two of the best salespeople he knew in the industry and started his own finance company—in his basement. Using a combination of direct mail and cold calls to attract customers, he and his commission-only team built up a $3 million a year business within three years. He didn't have to pay rent or salaries. His only overhead was buying lists, mailing marketing letters, and phone and Internet costs. After about five years, he had accumulated enough wealth that he could pay cash to send his kids to college, buy a beach house, and work as a volunteer the rest of his life.

The primary challenge of running this kind of business is that you are competing against other, similar businesses. You must out-hustle your competitors to stand apart. Guerrilla marketing becomes a must, and you need to make attracting customers your top priority. You also need a strong marketing message and memorable brand, great service, and a stream of testimonials and referrals from raving customers.

The remainder of this section provides you with an action plan to get started quickly in a business, followed by a second plan to grow your business into something larger than just yourself.

ACTION PLAN TO GET STARTED

1. Choose a service that you will enjoy offering to customers.

2. Prepare yourself mentally to dominate the market. The LFC/LBE business is a hustle business, meaning you have to outwork and outthink your competitors. You need to market harder than they do, look more professional, provide more consistent and reliable service, and delight your customers beyond anything the competition does.

3. Check local laws about licensing and bonding requirements, if any, for that business. Also, check with an insurance broker about reasonable insurance coverage for the business.

4. Get a bookkeeping program like Quickbooks, along with a bookkeeper who can help you keep your accounts if you don't have the skill or just don't want to take it on. Make sure you ask the bookkeeper to educate you about the key accounting statements and how to read them, if you don't already know.

5. Develop a name that is memorable and do a search online to be sure that no one has already taken the name. Visit your state department of business and the US Trademark Office online to be sure you are not infringing on an existing name in your specific business category. Check the Internet and make sure you can reserve the domain name for that business.

6. Develop a tagline or slogan that sets your service apart from anyone else. In marketing, this is called a Unique Selling Proposition, or USP. For instance, "Master's Plumbing Service: Boston's most professional, cleanest, and on-time plumbers." Or, "Maria's Catering: Southern-style BBQ smoked for hours, with a famous sauce made from scratch."

7. Rough out some numbers to determine how many customers you need every month to break even, to cover your living expenses, and to earn enough to replace and exceed your current income. Set some aggressive goals for achieving the level of income you want from your business.

8. Offer a guarantee that removes any concerns prospects might have in hiring you. For instance: "We get it right the first time or you don't pay."

9. Invest a bit of money in a logo that would make a franchisor proud. That way, your business has a professional feel to it, as opposed to many fly-by-night competitors.

10. Write up a policy-and-procedures manual that details exactly how you will provide the same level of service to customers every time. You can adjust the manual as your business evolves. However, start now so that you have a proprietary methodology that you can use to train employees down the road and make your company more valuable.

11. Test and roll out at least five marketing tactics every month to become increasingly visible. Every guerrilla marketer knows dozens of low-cost tactics: signs on the road, flyers, free publicity, referrals from your network, joining local associations and organizations, putting a large sign on your car, your Web site, low-cost directories, low-cost local advertising, writing articles, getting interviewed on local radio shows, leaving your business card and special offers near cash registers of non-competing businesses, and hundreds more. The original Guerrilla Marketing series of books will show you the way.

12. Go out of your way to delight customers.

13. Ask for referrals from every satisfied customer.

14. Follow up with customers to make sure they continue to call you when they have a need. Make sure they know how to reach you. Call them when it is time for service again or, better yet, schedule an appointment for a follow up after every visit.

15. Build a support network of friends, family, and other business owners who can help you stay passionate and motivated, even during challenges.

ACTION PLAN TO BUILD THE BUSINESS AFTER INITIAL SUCCESS

1. Market your business until you have all the customers you can handle and have no choice but to expand the business beyond just you. Do this by constantly testing and rolling out new marketing tactics. Also, set specific goals to determine the revenues and profits of the business. That way, you can grow the business on your terms. Set targets for the number of leads you will generate each month, the percentage of leads that will convert to customers, how much a first-time customer will buy, the number of purchases your customer will make every year, the dollar volume of each purchase, your gross profit margin, your cash flow, and your fixed costs. Set other goals as appropriate for your business, for instance: the percentage of customers who take you up on offers for add-ons and up-sells, as in McDonald's famous query, "Do you want fries with that?" If you don't achieve a goal, learn what went wrong and make a mid-course correction. If you do achieve your goal, raise it for the next month and develop tactics for hitting your target!

2. Develop the right attitude. A company-builder thinks differently than a sole proprietor. Think about what you need to do to have the business run without you at least for a few weeks at a time. Be willing to trust other people to grow the business for you, assuming you give them proper training and support. Keep your ego under control so that you don't need to be the hero who fights all the fires and solves all the programs.

3. Read, study, and get coaching about building your business. You're not the first person to launch a business, not by far. Fortunately, there are tons of books that can help you along the way, written by experts like Jay Conrad Levinson, Michael Gerber, Jim Collins, and Paul Hawken, whose *Growing a*

Business is an oldie but goodie. Also consider hiring a business coach to help you grow the business.

4. Detail every single major process that your company does, especially the processes that interact with customers. Lay out the steps and metrics that tell you whether a step has been done according to your standards. Assume you are teaching a sixth-grader. This is a crucial thing to do, because it frees you up to train your employees and grow the business. It also adds valuable intellectual property to your business. If you want to sell, the buyer knows that you have consistent processes in place and that the business can run on its own.

5. Put automation in place wherever possible to make the work easier. For instance, implement a customer database, automatic invoicing, and online newsletters that are sent automatically via autoresponders to customers and prospects. Similarly, launch an automatic marketing plan that tells you exactly what to do every day to make the business more visible and increase sales.

6. Set goals for when you can replace yourself by hiring other people to own different processes and functions in your business. Start saving cash reserves to be able to afford to hire new employees as the business grows and achieves its goals. Map out an organizational chart that would replace the non-CEO activities you currently do. For instance, if you are selling, add a box for a salesperson. If you are mowing lawns in your landscaping service, add a box for a head landscaper.

7. Hire only the most passionate, talented people for your company. Don't merely fill vacancies with anyone who can fog a mirror, even when demand for labor is tight. Look for people who love the work you are doing and fit your values. Set specific, measurable goals to hold every new employee accountable. If they don't meet your expectations after you give them training, tools, and sufficient time to improve, replace them.

8. Give the most talented people in your growing company the chance to take on added responsibilities and build the company. Reward them accordingly.

9. Consider starting an internal university in your company to train employees on best practices in your field. This will make your company stand out from other employers and help you become a magnet for top talent.

10. Keep raising standards and improving processes.

11. Once your company reaches the point where it is running on its own, you have many lucrative options available to you. You can franchise it. You can buy struggling competitors for a good price and convert them to the practices your business follows. You can open up new markets. You can get into related services that your current customers would value. Keep moving forward and don't look back!

CHAPTER 33

THE ANTI FLIP-THE-SWITCH BUSINESS—
The Long, Patient Way to a Bulletproof Career

I f you are in your twenties, thirties, or perhaps early forties, you have an opportunity that many of your older colleagues have squandered. Study after study reveals that a sizeable percentage of Americans have less than $10,000 saved for retirement. This fact is appalling—and embarrassing to me as an American. A nation built on the concept of personal responsibility is now populated by citizens who have not planned for retirement or a longer lifespan, even with tools and information at their disposal to do so.

Because you have time on your side, you can avoid this mistake. You can be ready to retire on your terms—if you are patient, if you have the discipline to keep the long view in mind, and if you are not tempted to keep up with your neighbors acquisition by acquisition.

Building the Anti Flip-the-Switch Business requires you to treat your household as a business and investment fund. YOU are the business. Your job is to invest every penny that comes into your household in order to earn a return. You keep your costs low, per the earlier chapter about getting your financial house in order, and generate a surplus that you invest wisely so that it grows over time.

Following are the steps to make this business a success:

1. Figure out how much money is enough for you to live on today. Create a lean, mean budget that takes care of your family's needs for shelter, clothing, transportation, and healthcare. Eliminate the luxuries that you know you don't need. Get rid of any expenses related to status and prestige.

2. Calculate how much money you need to have saved to be able to retire. There are dozens of free calculators on the Internet, including a suite of free tools for you at www.bulletproofcareer.com. Run some different scenarios. For instance, get a sense of what it will take with and without Social Security.

See what happens if you live on 75 percent, 100 percent, 150 percent or 200 percent of your current living expenses; remember that your expenses tend to rise as you get older and raise a family. Learn how the numbers change if you retire at different ages, like fifty-five, sixty, sixty-five, seventy, and seventy-five. Figure out how your situation will change if the government raises tax rates.

3. Run numbers to determine how much you need to put away every month to hit your goal, assuming a 5-percent, 8-percent, and 10-percent rate of return on your investments.

4. Adjust your budget accordingly in order to be able to save money at the required rate for you to hit your number. Use some of the more conservative scenarios to plan your budget. As suggested in an earlier chapter, if you are single, then cut costs so you can live on half your salary. If you are married, then live on only one spouse's income. Avoid the big expenses like new cars, a big house, private school for your kids, luxury vacations, taking care of dogs or cats for their lifetime, and eating out every night. You don't have to live like a monk, but try to find low-cost ways to enjoy time with friends and family. Save as much as you can.

5. Take time to learn about legitimate investment strategies, such as ETFs, aggressive index funds, annuities with guaranteed returns, and low-cost, diversified mutual funds. While equities have been horrific during the first decade of the twenty-first century, over the long haul, they remain the best way to grow your money. Work with an investment advisor that you trust for objective advice and for help getting into investments that match your risk profile.

6. Implement other low-risk income strategies to supplement your current income, such as publishing online information, moonlighting as a freelancer/consultant, or starting a side business that you can run on weekends. Pour proceeds from these efforts into your retirement fund.

7. Consider buying one investment property every couple of years. Only invest if you can put down a sizeable down payment and are sure that a 75 percent rental rate will cover your costs. Real estate has had a historic bust, but you can still make money in real estate by buying smart. Know your market and patiently look for deals. If you buy one profitable investment property every other year from the time you are thirty until you are fifty, you can have a

multimillion-dollar portfolio paying for itself and building equity for your retirement. Many of my friends have partially funded their retirement by investing in real estate over time. Some own rental homes, small industrial or commercial properties, and even public storage complexes. As I write this, they are buying additional properties to take advantage of the foreclosure and short sale situation. None of them do deals anywhere near the scale of Donald Trump, but they are patient, disciplined, long-term investors.

8. Don't cave in. Your time horizon with this strategy is decades, and so you have to be patient and disciplined. When you put money away for the future, don't touch it. When you really want to buy that new pair of shoes or lease the fancy car, don't do it. When you feel pressured to do something your neighbors are doing, don't. It is much better to have a friend with a boat than to actually own a boat! Keep living simply, saving and investing until you never have to worry about career security again.

CHAPTER 34

THE AGILE INTERIM EXECUTIVE OR MANAGER

I n this economy, every executive and manager works on an interim basis. The tenure of executives is so short and tenuous that it is hard to think of their employment in any other terms. At the same time, there is increasing demand for executives and managers to join an organization for a set time period and then either transition to a permanent role or move on.

Interim executives are especially in demand in the following situations:

- A key employee takes sick, maternity, or other form of leave, and a replacement is needed until the employee returns.

- A key employee is abruptly fired or leaves, and an immediate replacement is needed to maintain stability in the company or unit.

- A startup venture needs an interim executive or team of executives to get the company up and running before turning control over to a permanent team.

- An organization needs to turn itself around, and it hires an interim executive to make tough decisions.

- A scandal rocks an organization and an interim executive is needed to stabilize the situation.

- A company wants to try out a new manager or executive before committing to a full-time job offer.

- A buyout team wants to bring in a new executive or executive team on an interim basis to meet key milestones after an acquisition.

- The organization has an initiative with a finite start and end, like a product launch or software installation, and needs an interim manager with specific expertise to lead the project.

Interim executives can be hired internally or come from outside, depending on the needs of the organization. There are some wonderful benefits to working on an interim basis:

- **Compensation.** IInterim executives often receive a better compensation package than full-time employees, because it is understood that they have downtime when they are not being paid. You can also negotiate housing, car, bonus for performance, and, in some cases, health benefits. In my own case, in addition to a paycheck, I have also occasionally received stock and stock options as part of my compensation package.

- **Flexibility.** You can work six months out of the year and do what you want the rest of the time.

- **Choice.** You choose your assignments.

- **Variety.** You keep learning and moving on to new organizations with new challenges.

- **Compelling assignments.** Typically, you get hired to handle pressing issues that an organization faces. You get exposure to fascinating situations and problems.

- **Travel.** If you like to travel, being an interim executive is one way to see different parts of your country or the world. Alternatively, if you live in an area with a high concentration of companies in your niche, you don't have to travel if it's not your preference.

- **The opportunity to assess fit before you sign up full time.** Interim roles offer you a way to test out a company and position before you commit to a more permanent role. Of course, the client may be testing the waters as well.

- **Deeper access to the opportunity flow.** Interim executives typically get connected to top executives in an industry along with key sources of capital. Once you are recognized as an interim executive who performs well, people will provide you with an ongoing stream of opportunities.

Nancy McAward exemplifies the successful interim executive. A seasoned nursing executive, she has worked in leadership roles for major health systems across the country. She is gifted at understanding and navigating the culture of a complex health system, building alliances with staff and administrators, and rapidly improving performance in units. Now living in Florida within walking distance of her grandchildren, she alternates time at home with time on the road as an interim nursing executive. She finds assignments via a recruiter with whom she has worked for years, as well as through calls she receives from C-level executives that she knows. Her assignments have included helping a health system integrate a smaller health system that it acquired; turning around a hospital on the brink of bankruptcy; improving clinical quality and safety at a hospital after the abrupt departure of a chief nursing officer; and serving as interim nursing executive at a major health system. According to Nancy, the key challenge of the interim executive is "understanding the culture and the personalities, and getting results quickly in each new setting."

In my own experience as a management consultant, sometimes clients want more than consulting. For instance, I worked with an investment banker who had invested in an emerging debit card technology company. The company needed immediate capacity to market its products and implement its strategy. At the investment banker's advice, I served as the interim vice president of marketing for three months in order to build up the company's marketing collateral, Web site, call center, and distribution channels. The company understood that I had other business interests, such as my online publishing ventures and consulting, and agreed that I could continue to manage all non-competing interests outside of my work responsibilities. After I completed my milestones, I moved back to consulting and growing my online businesses.

If you wish to get interim assignments, take the following actions as appropriate for your situation:

- Do an online search of recruiters who specialize in interim executive placement.

- State your interest in interim assignments on your Web site and social-networking, professional profiles.

- Get to know people who place interim executives in your industry, especially investment bankers, venture capitalists, private equity investors, and people who sit on boards.

- Look for interim opportunities in industry journals.

- Register for interim opportunities on online sites dedicated to interim work, like my site: www.interimrevolution.com.

- If you do top-level consulting work, keep your antennae up for opportunities to do interim work.

- Look for job openings on online sites and offer to act in an interim role while the organization fills the position on a permanent basis. You might even get the offer for the permanent role.

- Put together a team of professionals with complementary skills, including finance, marketing, technology, human resources, and operations. Market your group as an interim startup team to investors and venture fund managers.

CHAPTER 35

GO GLOBAL!

n almost any career, overseas experience can provide invaluable contacts, knowledge, skills, and exposure. Looking abroad for opportunities can also help you avoid negative economic trends in your own country, like a declining dollar, increasing government deficits, and greater government involvement in the United States. Many employers value international experience and, if you have an entrepreneurial streak, you can find business opportunities in emerging countries. Whether you currently want to go overseas or not, at least consider your options and what it would take to add international experience to your resume. That way, going global can become one more backup plan you have in case you want or need to make a change.

There are many ways to go global, depending on your employment situation, family background, language skills, and where you are in your life:

- **Pick up and go.** If you don't have a family to support, have some cash, and want some adventure, you can move to another country and see what kinds of opportunities you can drum up. Stay with a friend who lives overseas. Learn the language if you need to. Immerse yourself in the culture. Research visa requirements and look for a job, or teach your local language for a fee. Look out for business opportunities as you learn more about the country. You read earlier about my friend who did exactly that by moving to Hong Kong shortly after college. He learned Mandarin while working at a low-paying job for the local satellite television monopoly. Meanwhile, he reached out to American firms and offered to help them navigate Hong Kong and China as they sought to expand there. Now he runs a successful venture firm focused on Asia.

- **Get a summer internship or grant.** If you are a student, why not find work overseas during the summer? I worked in Ecuador for Dole Fresh Fruit for the summer during my two-year MBA program despite having nearly hopeless Spanish-speaking skills. It was a wonderful chance to learn about international business and explore the agribusiness industry. While I didn't continue with Dole, a classmate of mine did, and he became a country director in Costa Rica before moving on as a sought-after executive in the agribusiness industry. Similarly, during my last summer of college, I received a grant to study micro-businesses in Nairobi while working with an international aid organization.

In both cases, the career office of my school provided information about these opportunities, and that was long before the Internet existed to provide even more information about internships, grants, and other overseas opportunities.

- **Volunteer.** If you have the time and money, you might find a number of organizations that will take you on as a volunteer overseas.

- **Pay for an overseas experience.** Organizations like Earthwatch created a market for people willing to pay for a fascinating work experience overseas. In the case of Earthwatch, you can pay to enjoy research and environmental conservation experiences.

- **Study abroad.** Take a year or two to study in another country. Many universities have sister schools abroad that allow students to attend for a semester or more.

- **Get global companies as consulting clients.** I was fortunate to land an assignment with a multinational coaching firm that hired me to train their coaches in Bali, England, and Melbourne. Similarly, a colleague of mine travels every month to France, Norway, Sweden, and the Netherlands to work with his consulting clients. However, you can get international gigs without ever having to travel. Around 40 percent of my Center for Executive Coaching members are from outside the United States, representing twenty countries. They participate in the program via distance learning, and we speak whenever needed via the free Skype calling service. Once you are on the Internet, whether with your own Web site or through listings services like elance.com and guru.com, you will be amazed at how far-ranging your clients can be.

- **Get an expatriate package.** If you work for a global company, request an assignment overseas. In many companies, overseas experience is a prerequisite for senior leadership, and only up-and-coming leaders are eligible for consideration. With an expatriate package, you get the advantage of a high salary versus local wages and housing allowances. These packages are less prevalent than they were in the past but still exist. At the same time, if you are offered an overseas assignment before you are ready, don't just balk at it. Listen to the offer. Consider how it can help you if you take it, and how it might hurt you if you don't. Be open to any overseas offer you receive, because you can't anticipate the opportunities it might open up for you.

- **Develop import relationships.** If you run a company or are in charge of procurement, you can get overseas experience by sourcing products and services from overseas. As you scale up, you can visit your suppliers to inspect them and build the relationship. For instance, my wife's company, Moms on Edge, manufactures some of her products in China and imports them. She has grown the company just about to the point where it makes sense to plan trips to meet with our overseas manufacturers.

- **Develop export relationships.** You can also go global by exporting your products overseas. Many independent reps overseas might want to represent your products and services and sell them in their local markets. Your company Web site should invite interested parties to contact you. In the case of my wife's business, a relative of one of her friends happened to be a distributor in Wales. He began searching for distribution arrangements with retailers there. You never know where an international relationship will form for you, as long as you keep up your relationships and let people know about what you are doing.

- **License your intellectual property or technology.** If you sell information or technology, you can sell the rights to your intellectual capital overseas. I am in discussions to license my Center for Executive Coaching, Boxing Fitness Institute, and other proprietary programs with people from Australia, Colombia, Mexico, China, and South Africa. With a strong Web site that invites people to contact you about licensing, you will get offers.

- **Set up a branch office.** Assuming you find someone you trust to run an overseas branch, you can set up a branch office in another country and expand your business presence that way.

- **Start an outsourcing company.** Love it or hate it, outsourcing will remain a trend as long as wages are so different across nations. Why not take advantage? For instance, many Web site and Search Engine Optimization firms now have relationships overseas with low-cost developers. For $10 per day, they hire a full-time Search Engine Optimization expert who has the equivalent of a Master's Degree. Companies outsource accounting, financial analysis, software programming, customer service, human resources administration, and manufacturing. You can become an expert on outsourced providers, and either broker outsourced talent or start a company that provides outsource services directly.

- **Take advantage of family contacts.** A friend of mine with family in India started a call center based there. He handles the marketing in the United States while his family handles operations overseas. The company received millions in venture funding and has landed some high-profile clients who wanted to outsource their call centers. If you have family overseas, reach out to them and come up with ways you can do business together.

- **Broker relationships between your country and businesses in other countries.** Once you get to know another country, you can broker relationships and take a percentage of any deals that are consummated by you. For instance, help bring successful U.S. franchises over to an emerging country.

- **Create a virtual global firm.** Going global doesn't mean you have to work overseas. I have no employees and yet work with a network of consultants and freelancers from around the world. These professionals, most of whom I have never met in person, handle all sorts of projects for me and come from Russia, Romania, India, Malaysia, China, and Thailand. Thanks to alibaba.com, elance.com, guru.com, and dice.com you can create your own virtual company, too. That way, you get the best talent worldwide at the best prices.

CHAPTER 36

FINESSE A CHANGE IN INDUSTRY, FUNCTION, OR COMPANY CULTURE

uppose your industry collapses within months, as happened to mortgagors, real estate brokers, and home-builders in recent times. How would you convince an employer in a different industry that you have transferable skills and the flexibility to make the switch? Or, consider the possibility that you might stop enjoying the work you do in your current function and want to try something different such as a switch from marketing to sales or from financial analysis to operations. How would you persuade a prospective employer, or a manager in your current company, that you can be successful in a new function? Finally, let's say that you work for a huge company and want to get experience in a smaller and more rapidly growing organization. How would you convince an entrepreneurial firm-owner that you can handle his very different culture? Or, if the reverse were true, how would you convince the executive at a massive corporation that you will thrive in a slower, more methodical and bureaucratic culture?

A big part of the answer is: finesse. You should already have relationships or be building connections that can help open doors for you. You are already competent and have skills and knowledge of value to offer, and you continue to add to the value you provide. Now you need the finesse to persuade potential clients or employers that they would be foolish not to hire you, even if the position represents a break from your past and their usual way of thinking. While some roles are out of reach until you have the required training, it is easier than you might think to make a relatively dramatic break from your industry, function, or company culture.

Here are three examples:

- **Case One: Functional change.** After five years working as a management consultant, I had had enough. I was getting married and didn't want to keep flying out of town four or five days every week. Around the same time, I recognized that I wanted to enter the world of writing, teaching, and training. In one of the luckiest breaks of my career, it turned out that the head of our firm's professional development and training function was leaving. I immediately called a number of partners in the firm who knew and supported me. I made the case to them to let me take over that role. I emphasized that I had deep on-the-ground experience about what it took to delight clients and could help our consultants be more successful with this knowledge. At the same time, they shared that they wanted to make significant improvements to our training and development function. We developed a vision of what that meant, and they hired me to implement this new vision. I was able to work from my home office while doing something I loved, even in a new function.

- **Case Two: Change to a completely new and emerging function.** An information technology manager I'll call David worked for a Fortune 500 consumer goods company. He was a top performer in his role. He also had an interest in environmental sustainability. When the company created a new office of sustainability as part of its corporate social responsibility initiatives, David asked if he could head it up. He did this even though he had no previous experience outside of information technology. The company liked the idea of assigning the role to someone who understood its culture and gave him the opportunity. David joined associations devoted to sustainability, enrolled in a distance-learning environmental policy program at a major university, and began to assess where his company was at in terms of standard environmental metrics. Now he is working to bake sustainability into the fabric of the organization. David turned his passion for sustainability and his knowledge of his company into an entirely new and, for him, satisfying career direction.

- **Case Three: Making a change to a new industry.** While I led the training and development role in my consulting firm, my new boss, the vice president of Human Resources, was plotting his own career path. He had come to our company to clean up our human resources policies so the firm could be sold. Seeing his work coming to an end, he decided that he wanted to shift into a different industry. Through his university alumni network, he learned about an executive position in the Human Resources department of a leading Silicon Valley chip-maker. His new title would be Director of Human Resources, a step down from his current title of vice president, but he would have responsibility for tens of thousands more employees in a much larger and more prominent company. He convinced the key decision-makers in the company that he could transfer his deep knowledge of Human Resources in the consulting and healthcare industries to his new role. He got the job, along with a compensation package that included generous stock options. He has since become a very wealthy man.

Finesse combines the perspectives of the influencer and the improviser described in the second part of this book. Having finesse means that you can persuade people that you are right for a position, even if you may not seem like a perfect fit. In other words, emphasize your strengths and turn any perceived weaknesses into strengths. For instance:

- If you don't have industry experience, explain how your deep functional knowledge brings value to your new employer, and how your past experience offers a fresh perspective.

- If you don't have expertise in a particular function, talk about how your existing skills will contribute, for instance, by making the function more efficient or responsive to customers.

- If you want to move from a small company to a bigger one, show how you can bring entrepreneurial energy and resourcefulness to the role.

- If you want to work at a smaller company, tell your potential employer about how you can implement systems and build capacity.

- If you are competing against other people with more traditional backgrounds, you can also turn their perceived strengths into weaknesses. For example, talk about how the industry is changing and needs fresh ideas. Note that you are in a better position to see things in a new way, especially compared to people who have worked in the industry during their entire career.

Take a moment and think about likely or appealing transitions you might make to a different industry, function, or company culture. List the strengths you have that you know can make you valuable compared to more traditional candidates. List the weaknesses you have, and how you can use finesse to turn those into strengths. That way, when you decide that it is time to make a shift, you are prepared. You can demonstrate why your prospective employers would be foolish not to at least give you serious consideration.

CHAPTER 37

BECOME DEAN OF YOUR PRIVATE CAREER UNIVERSITY AND USE THE BACK-TO-SCHOOL TRUMP CARD

f you have read this far, you know that ongoing learning and development is a constant theme in this book and a requirement for career longevity. This chapter focuses specifically on advancing your formal education.

In order to be agile, think of yourself as the dean of your own custom university. You must develop your own curriculum to stay fresh on your career path and be ready with the skills you need, in case you have to or want to make a shift. Learn what you need from current assignments, from mentors, and from training programs that your company or industry association offers. When these aren't sufficient, do some self-study, ask experts for advice, and get some coaching. At some point, perhaps more than once in your career, you may also find value by completing an advanced degree or certificate program at a university.

The facts are clear. You need an advanced degree to be credible in the workforce and earn top dollar. According to the Bureau of Labor Statistics, a professional with an advanced degree earns roughly $15,000 more per year than an employee with a bachelor's degree. This earnings gap grows to $22,000 compared to those with some college or an associate's degree, $27,000 compared to people with a high school diploma and no college, and almost $46,000 for those with less than a high school diploma. Unemployment rates are also lower when you have more education. As of February 2010, unemployment was 5 percent for those with a bachelor's degree and higher, 8.0 percent for those with some college or an associate's degree, 10.5 percent for those with a high school diploma and no college, and 15.6 percent for those with less than a high school diploma.

When I was going to school in the late 1980s, there were many fewer options than there are today for getting an advanced degree. You had to leave your job, pack up yourself and perhaps your family, and spend a couple of years on campus. My friends and I called this opportunity the back-to-school trump card. To us, it was a way to break out of a dead-end career or wait out a tough economy. In dire cases, it was like the Get Out of Jail Free card in Monopoly.

You can still play the back-to-school trump card, but play it wisely. If you work for a large employer, the organization may pay for some or all of your advanced education, if you agree to return to work for a specified period of time. Warning: the penalties can be stiff if you don't return. Think carefully before you sign up for what could become a Faustian bargain.

Regardless of whether your employer pays or you do, make sure you know exactly why you are going back to school and what opportunities you want to create for yourself while you are there. The people who thrived after graduation from my business school class were the ones who came to the MBA program with a plan. They focused their time in school on the activities and relationships that would help them achieve their goal. For example, one business school classmate was passionate about organic farming. He spent his time in business school working with a leading agribusiness expert and developing a business plan to start an international organic farming venture after graduation. Immediately after school, he raised money and launched his plan. Another classmate wanted to raise money to buy a business. He spent his two years developing a search plan and recruiting investors. Sure enough, within a year of graduation he bought a manufacturing company. A third had come from the military and, for whatever reason, had always loved the big cereal companies. He spent his time learning about consumer marketing and landed a job with one of the major consumer packaged-goods companies, working as a brand manager on a leading children's cereal.

Meanwhile, the people who didn't have a plan and were simply escaping from their previous job didn't do as well. They got some attractive job offers, but because they didn't have specific goals and didn't know themselves as well as they should have, they tended to flounder after graduation, bouncing from job to job. Many seemed to be just as unfulfilled as they were before going to school. Yes, I was in this category, and it took me almost a decade to figure out who I was, what I love to do, and how to build a successful career doing it. The moral: most people only get to play the back-to-school trump card once, so play it smart!

Today you don't have to pack up and go to school for a couple of years in order to get that advanced degree. Almost every top college and university now offers virtual degree programs, some of which are 100 percent online while others require a manageable chunk of time on campus. You can also complete some fascinating and valuable certificate programs. These might not come with a formal degree, but they can advance your career. One of the most useful certificate programs I ever took was an e-commerce course through UC Berkeley's adult education program. In other words, there is no excuse not to continuously develop and upgrade your knowledge, skills, and credentials.

This chapter ends with a cautionary tale. A regional health system determined that in order to remain leading edge and competitive in their market, their nurse managers needed to be master's-degree prepared in nursing and/or business. Too many of their nurses had the minimum credential required, and that wasn't good enough in the highly complex and technical healthcare industry. The health system gave incentives to nurse managers and aspiring nurse managers to advance their education, and constantly reinforced the need for them to enroll in a program. After a year or so of this program, they promoted only those nurse managers who took their message to heart and were matriculating in advanced-degree programs.

Despite this support, around 25 percent of the nurse managers still refused to participate to earn an advanced degree. They claimed they didn't have the time or didn't see the need. Some were simply afraid to go back to school after being out for so many years. Now they are stuck in the same positions, without the potential for a pay raise. They are vulnerable to layoffs, too, because other health systems in the area have adopted similar requirements.

Don't be like these nurses. Take advantage of the huge number of educational opportunities available to you. Try to always be enrolled in at least one training, certificate, or degree program. Set aside time for ongoing training and education to achieve your career development goals. Make it a priority over watching television at night or sleeping late on weekends. Even as the cost of education and training rises, ongoing professional education usually pays for itself over the long term.

CHAPTER 38

RECHARGE AND REINVENT YOURSELF WITH A SABBATICAL

eave open the possibility of taking a sabbatical to travel the world, test out entirely new career directions, or cross off some of the items on your bucket list. During a terrible economy, a sabbatical can be a way to take cover, gain new life experiences, and emerge recharged and ready to be productive when the economy turns around again. Alternatively, if you feel like you are burning out in your present role, a sabbatical can help you figure out what you want to do next in life. It can also give you a way to reconnect with family, find more meaningful work, regain your spontaneity and creativity, launch a lifestyle business, or simply take a break.

There is a surprising amount of information available about sabbaticals. If you search "take a sabbatical" on Google, you will find 1.3 million results. At the top of your search you will meet Clive Prout, who has established a niche as The Sabbatical Coach and has even trademarked that title. Clive works with successful individuals who have discovered that success didn't bring them the happiness they expected. He helps them find what he calls "their new dream." For him, a sabbatical is not just about taking time off and then returning to the same job. It is about creating a new vision that is in line with one's values, even if that means a dramatic change in work and lifestyle.

Clive should know, because he went through the same process. He used to work in high-technology marketing, living in an urban apartment complex. Now he lives on a small island off Washington State, resides in an eco-friendly cooperative housing community, and makes a living with his coaching practice.

He uses the term sabbatical loosely. Many high-profile executives and business owners can't easily extract themselves for months to travel the world. Therefore, he helps them create a weekend retreat or even a series of conversations to create the space they need to dream about doing something different and finding what they really want. He wants his clients to see new possibilities, figure out how they can make these possibilities become real, and begin to craft the life they really want.

If you continue to read through the Google results, you will find books about how to plan a sabbatical, including *Escape 101: The Four Secrets to Taking a Sabbatical or Career Break Without Losing Your Money or Your Mind* by Dan Clements and Tara Gignac; and *Six Months Off: How to Plan, Negotiate & Take the Break You Need Without Burning Bridges or Going Broke* by Hope Dlugozima, James Scott, and David Sharp. You will learn that some companies encourage employees to take occasional sabbaticals and even pay them to do so. There are hundreds of sites dedicated to planning a sabbatical, and many more blogs by people who are in the middle of, or have taken, a sabbatical. You will also learn about successful people who have taken sabbaticals: Liane Hansen of National Public Radio; Graham Birch of BlackRock, who went from overseeing $36 billion in assets to buying dairy and sheep farms in England; Bill Gates, who takes an annual sabbatical simply to think; and many artists, designers, authors, and scholars. Finally, you'll be reminded of Billy Crystal's character in the movie *City Slickers*. He takes a sabbatical on a dude ranch so that he can find joy again, despite a painful midlife crisis.

If you can dream, you can plan a sabbatical that fits your budget, goals, timeframe, and family situation. Take a moment and imagine a three-month, six-month, and one-year sabbatical. If you are not in a position to take time off, come up with a way to follow Clive Prout's format. Create a weekend retreat or engage in a series of conversations with a trusted colleague or a coach to come up with your new dream.

As you plan your sabbatical, answer these questions:

- What is causing you to want to take a sabbatical? Are you unfulfilled, directionless, in need of a break, seeking a new adventure, or something else?

- What questions about your life or career direction would you want to answer during your sabbatical?

- Are you looking to completely reinvent your life, or do you want to enjoy some time off and then get back to a life that is similar to your present situation?

- What specific goals would you want to achieve by the time you finish?

- What would make your time on sabbatical one of the most rewarding experiences of your life?

- What would you want to see, do, learn, and experience?

- Where might you go, if anywhere?

- Would you go alone or with others?

- If your sabbatical is more of a process than an actual trip, who do you want to meet or ask for advice?

- What budget can you set aside for your sabbatical?

- What kinds of resources, companies, and people can help you get more information about your specific sabbatical plan?

- How would you take care of your current responsibilities, such as paying bills and maintaining any property?

- What can you do to influence your employer to support your sabbatical—for instance, by reserving your spot in the company for when you return, if you want to?

- What would you need to do in order to reengage back to normal life, get a new job, and deal with the real world once again? How much time will you need to make the transition out of your sabbatical and to your next step?

If your answers to the above questions are compelling and exciting to you, set a timeline and make it happen! At the very least, have a sabbatical ready to go as a career backup plan, in case you get blindsided by bad news and don't know what to do next, or you simply want some time to recharge and reinvent yourself. It could be one of the most rewarding career moves you ever make.

CHAPTER 39

ADVANCED CAREER AGILITY:
Form an Acquisition or Start-up Team

With enough experience, you might feel ready and able to start up a groundbreaking new venture or acquire a company of some scale. You might be in your forties before you feel like you have the confidence, competence, and contacts to start something up. On the other hand, the founders of Google, Microsoft, Facebook, YouTube, Nike, and Nantucket Nectars would tell you that you can start in your teens and twenties.

Unlike the LFC/LBE business, a groundbreaking venture is potent enough to somehow change the rules of an industry or dominate the competition with a product that is better in some meaningful and significant way. It requires a talented management team, a clear and compelling profit model, an operations platform that can deliver results, and a unique and proprietary edge that no one else has. Often a venture like this requires far more money than you alone can provide. It might need help from friends and family, investors in the angel community, suppliers who are willing to invest, and/or venture capitalists.

The majority of new ventures fail. Even if a brilliant venture capitalist with a terrific track record funds your business, you still have less than a one in ten chance of hitting it big. Even then you might get kicked out of your business before it succeeds. Too often, the entrepreneur risks everything, including his or her life savings and family's future for an idea that never pans out. It's heartbreaking to see television shows like *Shark Tank* or *American Inventor* and meet people who are risking everything for an idea that seems silly to everyone else.

On the other hand, every once in a while an entrepreneur goes to the mat with an idea and wins. Fred Smith, founder of Federal Express, shipped fewer than seven packages on his first overnight run, despite investing $4 million in inheritance money and millions more in venture capital. After shutting down for a month to market and expand his shipping network, his next run handled fewer than two hundred packages. Smith almost lost everything in 1973, but he went to Las Vegas and won $27,000 in blackjack to keep his company going. By the late 1970s, nearly fifteen years after he wrote about his idea in an economics paper, which supposedly earned a C grade, his company finally became a recognized brand.

Similarly, James Dyson, pioneering inventor of the industry's leading vacuum cleaner, took a long, torturous road to achieve success. It took him thousands of prototypes, a major lawsuit, debt that would make most of us give up, and the guts to break some significant rules about marketing a consumer product.

While Dyson and Smith became legends, most stories do not end well. In my own network, a colleague licensed a can't miss, groundbreaking nanotechnology solution from a major university. He put his entire fortune into it and persuaded many of his friends and family to do the same. Unfortunately, when he tested his product at a larger scale than the university had, it didn't work. He lost everything, suffered a horrible divorce, and faces multiple lawsuits from his investors. Worse, because he failed to be transparent about the results of his testing, his reputation is now damaged—probably beyond repair.

It takes a special kind of person to go for the big idea. I've done it on a smaller scale than the individuals above, with the Mixed Martial Arts Business and a couple of e-commerce businesses, and never hit the jackpot. Now, I only invest in LFC/LBE businesses, and risk no more than $1,500 of my own money with any attempt. The rest comes from sales and good old-fashioned bootstrapping.

What's your risk profile? Is it worth it to you to bet everything on an idea that probably won't work out and could cost you your savings, your marriage, and your family's future? If so, go for it! If not, set a stop-loss and limit your exposure.

A second option for the more seasoned manager is to buy a company and earn a return by improving cash flow, paying down debt, and then reselling the company again at a profit. Private equity firms, hedge funds, and investment banks tend to dominate the market for buying mid-sized and large private companies, especially when credit markets are flowing and regulations are loose. It is not easy for a solo entrepreneur and his or her team to compete against these firms' access to the deal flow and their ability to move quickly to evaluate and close deals. Therefore, if you want to buy a relatively large company, consider joining one of these firms and rising up to the ranks of partner.

If you would like to buy a smaller company, say, in the less-than-$15 million-in-revenue range, you have a better chance as a solo investor. Other books go into depth about this strategy, and you can visit www.bulletproofcareer.com for a list of resources, which include these points:

- Focus your search criteria on a specific industry, company size, and type of company. That way, your search will be more efficient.

- Build a team that includes a strong CPA and an attorney with experience structuring deals. Depending on your own capabilities, recruit some seasoned executives ready to run all or part of any company you buy.

- Line up investors who have interest in participating in your deal. The stronger your power base, the more likely you are to find investors of the caliber you need. You might even recruit some investors to fund your search in exchange for a first look at—and sweetened terms on—any deals you find. These investors can also serve as an informal board of advisors who can help you find deals and give you advice.

- Develop a list of companies that meet your search criteria. Databases like Dun & Bradstreet, Hoovers, and InfoUSA, along with the Chamber of Commerce and association directories are good resources.

- Send letters out to companies that match your search criteria and ask them if they would be interested in selling.

- Develop a network of professionals who can connect you to owners who might want to sell, including business brokers, commercial bankers, business attorneys, financial planners who work with business owners, vendors to companies in your target market, and association executives.

- Set a deadline to find a company or move on to other pursuits. People who take this path sometimes discover that the experience of trying to buy a company opens up wonderful opportunities to join firms that focus on acquisitions. Even if you fail, you can still take your career to a new level simply by getting out there, stirring things up, and showing people that you have the guts to do big things.

CHAPTER 40

WHAT ABOUT JUST GETTING A
NEW JOB IN THE SAME FIELD?

A fter reading this part of the book, some of you may feel overwhelmed. You may be saying to yourself, "Wait a minute. I just want to move up the ladder in my current company, or progressively move up in my industry. My head is spinning with all of these options. It's too much!"

The options presented in this part of the book are not meant to overwhelm you. They are options for your consideration, to help you be agile and have one or more backup plans ready to go. You never know when you are going to be ambushed. As you have read more than once in this book, your company might have a severe setback within the next year that costs you your job, all for reasons you cannot currently anticipate or would never expect. Be ready to reinvent yourself at any time.

I sincerely hope that your current situation remains stable, fulfills you, improves your financial standing over time, and carries you all the way to a secure retirement. But don't bet on it.

Your first line of defense is your double spike, described early in this book. The first spike is the value of who you know. The second spike is what you know that also brings value to others. Ideally, you spike in both of these arenas and can always find a new, better situation based on your strengths.

Your second line of defense is career agility. You can minimize your risk and improve your upside by thinking about new forms in which to work: online publishing, consulting/freelancing, building a firm, starting a small business, investing in passive income over the long haul, going back to school, taking a sabbatical, and buying or starting a significant business venture. Some of these strategies are short-term ways to regroup and retool like school and sabbaticals; others are things you can do in your spare time until they can replace your income, including online publishing, moonlighting as a consultant, and investing; and still others can become new full-time occupations for you.

Depending on your tolerance for risk and whether or not you already own a company, you can choose one of the following three templates to be agile in your career.

One: the conservative approach. If you are fundamentally conservative and really like the concept of a job, then make sure your power base is filled with people who support you, can protect you in your current position, and can connect you to new opportunities if the need comes up. Plot out a career path to move up in your present company, while forging ever-stronger relationships within your company and with others in the industry. Meanwhile:

- Create and implement a professional development plan that includes specific educational and training opportunities that will keep you ahead of the curve.

- Save as much money as you can, and invest it wisely for your age and risk profile.

- Develop a plan to get into consulting, or work on an interim basis in case you get laid off or fired and can't find a new job.

- Be open to an international assignment if that is a requirement to move up at your company.

- At some point, if you feel ready, start networking with investors and entrepreneurs in the industry, so that you can evaluate opportunities to get involved in viable start-up ventures.

Two: the aggressive approach. If you are less attached to the concept of a job, then be ready for anything. You still need strong relationships in place and constant upgrades to your skills. In addition:

- Stay at a company as an employee only as long as you are learning, making great contacts, or have a clear path to get rich. Get into assignments that give you profit-and-loss responsibility, let you develop new products, or allow you to learn the market firsthand as a salesperson.

- Find opportunities at growing, mid-sized companies with between $20–$250 million in sales that are big enough to have resources and creative enough to be dynamic, but not so big that they are bureaucratic and stuck in their ways.

- Consider an international assignment in order to learn about an emerging market and opportunities there.

- On the side, test information products and other online ventures, moonlight as a consultant, and/or start a small business that you can run nights and weekends. Be sure to stay within the legalities of your employment contract and work for hire laws.

- If you don't already run a company, meet with entrepreneurs and investors in your industry and establish relationships with them. Have them see you as a dynamic leader with key skills and value so that they think of you when an opportunity comes up.

- Plan for sabbaticals and time to go back to school, but only when you have a specific purpose in mind.

Three: the established entrepreneur. If you already run your own business, grow it or watch it stagnate. As Andy Grove *(Only the Paranoid Survive)* suggests, get paranoid.

- Strengthen relationships with vendors, customers, bankers, entrepreneurs, and others in your industry. Don't burn bridges just because your business is successful today. Who knows about tomorrow?

- Think about all of the threats to your business and how you can fortify your business to be prepared.

- Anticipate opportunities and strengthen your business to take advantage of them.

- Consider possible changes to your customers and their needs, the competition, economic ups and downs, government intervention, suppliers, talent and the labor market, and technology. Prepare for these changes so that you stay ahead of your competitors. Keep playing out different scenarios and how your business can react.

- Build up cash reserves to survive during tough times.

- Grow the business through new products and services, more loyal customers, good people you can train to grow the business on your behalf, and strategies to dominate.

- Prepare a plan to make the business run without you, so that you can exit at any time.

- Know what you will do next if your business fails or you want out.

PART IV:

COMMON COMBAT SITUATIONS

CHAPTER 41

SEVEN STEPS TO SUCCESS DURING YOUR FIRST NINETY DAYS IN A NEW ROLE

Your first ninety days in a new job are crucial. During this time you confirm to your boss that he or she made the right call by hiring you, and you establish your reputation as an emerging top performer. Alternatively, you can make people question whether you have what it takes. Use the following seven-step plan to give the right impression and hit the ground running in a new role.

One: Clarify what success means in your new role. Get as specific and measurable as possible about what you are expected to achieve—and when. A job description sometimes doesn't go further than describing your responsibilities and the things that you do. It doesn't focus enough on results. Work with your boss to go beyond the job description and set specific goals, or what some companies call Key Performance Indicators, or KPIs. That way, there is no doubt about your accountability and how to measure your success. Set specific milestones starting with your first three months, six months, and full year on the job.

Two: Help your boss win. One guaranteed way to succeed in any organization is by helping your boss succeed. Even more important, never do anything to embarrass or undermine your boss. Understand your boss's personal and career aspirations and what he needs to do to succeed. What are the KPIs that define his success to his boss? What are his career goals? What drives him? Does he want to be rich, famous, or safe? How can you help him get more done with less hassle?

At the same time, study your boss's communication style and adapt to it. Does he want you to get to the bottom line and be concise, or does he need you to lead him through your recommendations step by step? How often does he want progress updates, and via what medium, like texts, e-mail, memos, voice mail, or face-to-face meetings? When problems come up, at what point does your boss want to get involved, and what proactive steps and recommendations does he expect from you?

Three: Learn the culture and fit in. Many organizations have strong cultures. They don't tolerate people who can't or won't fit in. Take time to understand the unspoken norms in your company. Otherwise, you risk being perceived as strange and will have trouble getting things done. What are the company values, and how can you be sure that your behaviors are in line? How are decisions made? Which behaviors get rewarded? What is the tolerance for risk? What are expectations about dress, socializing, and work ethic? What are differences in what the company says versus what it actually does? Who are the quirky people who don't quite fit in, and how can you avoid following in their footsteps?

Four: Align yourself with the key players. Take the perspective of the politician to figure out who has power in the organization, and why they have it. Develop a strategy to understand their aspirations and help them succeed. Get involved in the most visible initiatives. Do all of this without alienating your boss or breaking the chain of command.

Five: Avoid political landmines. Every organization has sensitive issues and sacred cows. While it might be wise to take these on when you have more authority and your role is secure, don't step on these landmines in your first ninety days. For instance, don't take sides in a feud between two executives. Avoid conflicts in general. Don't get involved in a controversial project that has weak support from the top. Don't tell your boss that his strategy, or the company's strategy, is wrong.

Six: Take enough time to observe and assess before taking action. Clarify with your boss how much time you have to learn about the organization, understand the issues relevant to your role, and form relationships before you are expected to make decisions and really get things done. For instance, Pastor Timothy Riggs has developed a reputation for helping struggling churches turn around. In his book *The Church Leader Success Manual*, he shares that he spends up to eighteen months getting to know the people in a new church before he makes any significant decisions. It takes that long to understand the strengths of the people, the needs of the community, and how the church can thrive again. Few of us have eighteen months to start performing in a for-profit corporation, but Pastor Riggs's example is a perfect illustration of the need to take time to acclimate to your new position and organization.

Seven: Create a development plan to succeed in your new role. The title of Marshall Goldsmith's book, *What Got You Here Won't Get You There,* contains an ingenious truth for anyone taking on a new role. To succeed in your current role and continue to move up, you will likely need a new set of skills and way of managing. Take some time to create a development plan. Based on the requirements in your role and to move up to the next level, answer the following questions:

- Which assignments can give you the skills, exposure, and track record you need to succeed?

- Which people do you need to know? For instance, who would be good mentors to you? Who can help you navigate the organization? Who else besides your boss do you need on your side? What alliances do you need outside your unit to get things done? Would it make sense to hire an executive coach?

- What skills and knowledge do you need? What is the plan to acquire them? For instance, which training or educational programs will you take?

- Which new, more effective behaviors do you need to start making habitual? Which behaviors do you need to eliminate?

- What changes in your attitudes and perceptions might you need in order to be successful?

- What else will help you succeed in your role and get to the next level?

CHAPTER 42

ELEVEN CAREER SUCCESS PRINCIPLES FOR STUDENTS AND NEW GRADUATES

C hange and uncertainty create opportunities, especially for people new in their careers. While there are many trends that will make life more challenging for students and new graduates, there are also tremendous possibilities. Emerging technologies are creating entirely new industries, jobs, lifestyles, and career paths. The Internet, still in its infancy, continues to support new game-changing business models and ways of interacting. The aging population demands new services to care for their needs and wants. Continuing globalization presents opportunities for entrepreneurs to connect people and make global markets more efficient. Providing security to squash terrorist attacks, delivering quality healthcare, feeding billions of people and giving them access to clean water, finding alternative sources of clean energy at the right cost, and preserving the environment are also massive opportunities. If you are an optimist, there is no better time to be alive and starting a career, despite the gloom and doom that sells newspapers and gets us to watch television news.

To capture these opportunities, follow the guidance you have already read in this book and in the previous chapter about your first ninety days in a new position. At the same time, following are eleven success principles specifically for students and new graduates entering the workforce.

One: Make yourself marketable. A useful model is to become what one Fortune 100 company calls "T-shaped." The T-shape refers to individuals who are both deep and broad. They possess deep knowledge of a technical or functional field, as well as good written and verbal communication skills and a broad knowledge of business, history, politics, literature, and other liberal arts. They have worked successfully on multidisciplinary teams, know how to think critically, and can solve complex problems that may go beyond their discipline or major. They work well with other people and understand how to make persuasive recommendations about a course of action.

Two: Start building your network now. Your classmates today are the executives, investors, and politicians of tomorrow. Stay in touch with them. Take the time to get to know your professors. They can guide you to new opportunities and give you advice throughout your career. Look for mentors who support you and can help you understand less obvious aspects of how to get things done in your organization. Form relationships with talented coworkers. Turn your boss into a raving fan. Get active outside of work in industry associations so that people in your field see you as a leader.

Three: Don't obsess about what you have to be when you grow up, or believe you need to find a perfect first job. Lots of students almost drive themselves crazy believing that their first job out of school is a make or break proposition. It's not. You can learn and gain positive experiences from almost any situation, from minimum wage jobs to volunteer work. What's important now is that you learn who you are and what you want to do and, perhaps more importantly, figure out what you don't want to do.

Four: Have the guts and the spirit to try different, interesting things. Explore, especially while you are young and relatively unencumbered. Even if you have significant student loans, your life will only get more expensive and complex from here. You have much less to lose now than you will when you have a family and a mortgage, assuming that's part of your plan. Don't find yourself turning forty and looking back to realize that you never had the courage to take risks, go for a few dreams, and do the hard work needed to figure out who you really are.

Five: Live simply and frugally. The more flexible you are in your life, the easier it is for you to take advantage of once-in-a-lifetime opportunities you might attract. If career is important to you, do your best to stay single and without children until you at least establish yourself financially. Avoid buying lots of stuff that makes it hard for you to be flexible. Never have an unpaid credit card balance. Don't get a pet. Rent an apartment or buy a home that fits well within your budget.

Six: Perform. Don't expect your boss or anyone else to support you until you have demonstrated value and earned their trust. Get results in your job and the rest will follow. The better you perform and the more you contribute, the more you will get in return. Advancement follows from persisting despite setbacks and from learning how to make positive things happen in challenging situations. Many of your peers will quit when things get tough. Listen to your inner drill sergeant and stick it out! That kind of fortitude builds trust with your colleagues, strengthens relationships, and opens up new opportunities.

Seven: Have a good attitude. I'll never forget working with a new college graduate who was a complete disaster in his job. He made mistakes, missed deadlines, communicated unclearly, and went off on tangents while doing his work. Despite all of this, he had a fantastically positive attitude. He came early and stayed late, tried to help wherever he could, was an advocate for the company in the community and to potential new hires, and was pleasant to everyone. I overheard his boss say, "Normally I'd fire someone who makes as many mistakes as he does, but his attitude is so positive I'm willing to work with him and see if he can get there." In other words, a positive attitude not only helps you move ahead if you perform, it also gives you a measure of protection if you need it.

Eight: Milk your employer for knowledge and experience. Your real education begins when you graduate from school. Learn as much as you can from everyone you meet on the job. Take advantage of as much training as you can get. Observe the top performers and model yourself after them. Look for the most promising assignments, and get assigned to them. Keep assessing what you need to do or learn to keep progressing.

Nine: Take care of the details. It is extremely refreshing to work with new employees who show up on time, stay late, communicate professionally, keep their word, proofread their writing, and get things done. I'll never forget working with a new hire who sent the following e-mail out to some important clients: "The rooster is attached." She meant to write, "The roster is attached." Our clients got a good laugh from her gaffe, but not in a good way. The new hire gave them ammunition to wonder aloud why our fees were so high if we couldn't even be bothered to use spell-check. Watch the little things.

Ten: Adapt. Throughout your career, you probably will work for someone who is older than you, talks faster or slower than you, processes information differently from you, is more or less comfortable with technology than you, and has talents different from yours. You will notice these differences earlier in your career, especially if you are coming out of a school where most of your classmates are fairly similar to you. Be flexible. Learn to adapt to others' styles, while still having your own point of view. People like people who are more like them.

Eleven: Develop your own authentic voice. All sorts of people, including the authors of this book, are trying to influence you and give you advice. A partial list of people with their own agendas might include career politicians on either side of an issue, news publishers, celebrities who try to speak up about issues, advertisers, CEOs of huge corporations, self-proclaimed spiritual gurus, college professors in the social sciences and liberal arts, tort lawyers, and commission-based salespeople. Be very careful of us. Learn who you are as quickly as you can, and make grounded, considered decisions based on what your head, heart, gut, and spirit tell you.

CHAPTER 43

OPPORTUNITIES FOR THE STAY-AT-HOME MOM OR DAD

Stay-at-home parents have some terrific opportunities to create the lifestyle they want. You can moonlight with a part-time business that serves the people in your community, offer your freelance services to a worldwide market via sites like Elance, and set up an online business. Because online businesses are the newest opportunity for the stay-at-home parent, this chapter provides two examples of successful online mompreneurs. First, Jaden Hair created a food blog that earned money from advertising revenues, and then she grew her online presence into a way to earn multiple streams of income. Second, my very own wife, Elena, built a successful online presence by selling products and information focused on parenting and etiquette. Both businesses make money in different ways and exemplify classic online business models. Hopefully, these two pioneers will inspire you to take what you know and use it as the source to build your own home-based business.

Jaden Hair's Steamy Kitchen. When Jaden Hair moved to Sarasota, Florida, she missed the diversity and quality of restaurants, grocery stores, and food available in her former home in San Francisco. One night she found herself eating at a supposed Chinese restaurant called Bangkok Tokyo, a name having nothing to do with China, so she decided to act. In addition to teaching Asian cooking classes, she started recording family recipes online, often with her mother dictating them to her. She posted them on a blog at www.steamykitchen.com so her students could get to them and so she wouldn't lose them if her own computer crashed.

Three months later, Jaden realized she loved blogging. She decided to build a business blogging about Asian cooking. She tried to write a business plan but found the traditional business plan format too boring for her. Instead, she got out a bunch of magazines and poster board and created a collage of her vision of the business. She explains, "I hung it on my wall and it was the most inspiring thing I've ever done. It kept me focused on what I wanted to do, how I wanted to affect people, and how I wanted to feel. I created the business to be a mom, be at home, work from anywhere in the world if I wanted, and take my kids traveling with me if needed. I wanted to inspire people to feel good and to nurture them with food. I recommend that anyone uses a collage like this to keep focused and on track."

Part of Jaden's vision was to create a presence in many different media. She started small and with tenacity, like any guerrilla. For instance, she called the smallest local paper in her area, a free paper that was dropped off in everyone's driveway once a week. She told the editor that she would love to publish a recipe and a photo once a month at no charge, and they agreed. Then she moved up to a bigger free paper in town. After writing a column for them, she got a weekly column at the *Tampa Tribune*.

She did the same thing with television. First she called a small local affiliate. They took her call and invited her to come in. Then she started calling bigger and bigger stations. Now she has been on *Daytime* in a hundred markets, the *CBS Early Show*, Martha Stewart Radio, Oprah.com, and Forbes.com. "I learned the art of picking up the phone and calling," she shares. "I started small, got practice, and worked my way up. When it was time to call the *Today* show, it was easy for me to do."

Meanwhile, her online presence has grown significantly. She now gets more than half a million visitors every month and lucrative income from advertising revenues. She is in the top 600 worldwide in terms of Twitter influence. She has started a new Web site www.newasiancuisine.com to celebrate Asian Cuisine and also www.foodblogforum.com to share her knowledge of food and social media. It is no wonder that the Web site Slashfood.com named her one of the 10 Hottest Women in the Food Industry.

As a result of this platform, she has published a cookbook and has a second on the way. She has even landed the same agent as Paula Deen.

Jaden has the following advice for stay-at-home parents who want to become bloggers:

One: Be authentic. "I didn't start out to make money. Sharing recipes and teaching people how to cook was my identity. It was, and is, something that I really, really love and identify myself with. You have to be completely authentic in what you do. People can smell fakes and frauds. Do you love what you are writing about 100 percent? Can you talk about it all the time and work twenty hours in a row because you love it so much?" To keep her voice authentic online, Jaden uses dictation software called MacSpeech to write her blog posts, so that "My blog is my voice!"

Two: Find balance. "I have a good problem. I love creating recipes and testing recipes so much and have so much fun that most of the time I don't consider it work! I designed the business to be a stay-at-home mom, and I need to make sure I step away from the kitchen sometimes." To make sure her work is diversified, Jaden started only taking on projects that could involve her whole family and happen outside of the kitchen. "I'm just about to launch a travel section on SteamyKitchen.com, because that's something my entire family loves to do. We get to explore the world, I'll write about food and travel, and it's still part of my business."

Three: Diversify and be agile. "Technology moves so fast. Blogging could become passé like MySpace. Twitter might give way to Google Buzz. Online ads are half of my business; what if those go away? Everything could dry up in a matter of weeks, so you have to diversify. I use blogging, Twitter, television, print, radio, public speaking, and cookbooks. I constantly keep my eye on what's hot." The result is that Jaden is able to reach millions of people across multiple platforms, something incredibly valuable to her business and to product sponsors. "Brands like Scanpan, Hokto-Kinoko Mushrooms, and even the National Pork Board recognize the value of working with someone like me because there's a very high level of engagement that I have with my readers that stretches across print, online, and television. That's been the 'secret sauce' to my success."

Four: Surround yourself with people who are smarter than you. Jaden's husband Scott worked seven years with motivational speaker Tony Robbins. According to Jaden, "One of Robbins's life lessons that we both live by is, 'You are who you surround yourself with.' Based on that lesson, I sought out experts in writing, technology, and cooking and asked for their advice and mentorship." She wasn't afraid to ask for help, and doing so saved her time, frustration, and money, as she was able to learn from her mentors' lessons. Early on, Jaden sought advice from one of the most well-known food bloggers in the world, Elise Bauer of SimplyRecipes.com. "Her words of wisdom came from seven years of experience, priceless in our online world."

Five: Go diving for answers. Jaden says the most valuable tool in her business isn't her chef's knife or her favorite pan. It's the online search engine. When she first began her business, she didn't know the first thing about blogging software, HTML, CSS, SEO or any of the other technical gibberish that was required to be successful. In fact, she barely even knew how to operate her digital camera beyond pointing and clicking. Yet Jaden mastered those skills and more within months. She did it by diving for answers via search engines like Google.

Searching for "best blogging software" and "how to customize a Web site" led her to hundreds of Web sites full of valuable information and step-by-step tutorials. Resources like problogger.net and lynda.com gave her instant answers and a shortcut to trial-and-error.

Six: Give Back. "My fulfillment absolutely depends on gratitude and contribution," says Jaden. "I don't understand how the world works sometimes, but I know this for sure: I only get as much as I give." Her quick rise to fame was because of the generosity of experts like Elise Bauer, and newspaper editor Mike Eng for giving her a chance with her first column. Jaden is giving back in many ways. For instance, she recently banded with women in her area to lead a community garden project. "My mission is to teach kids that carrots don't come from a truck and to bring enjoyment of gardening and cooking with fresh ingredients to families in my community." Similarly, when Jaden kept getting emails from beginner bloggers asking for advice, she saw an opportunity to launch FoodBlogForum.com, a Web site dedicated to sharing tips, tools, and best practices. "There are so many components to food blogging: recipe development, writing, making food look pretty on a plate, and the entire technology side of social media. I wanted a place where people could come and learn and where I could spill my secrets to success, just as Elise had done with me when I began."

Elena Neitlich's Etiquette Empire. My wife, Elena, started her company Moms on Edge at www.momsonedge.com to get our kids to sleep. Working with a friend, she designed a prototype product made out of felt called the Goodnight Stoplight. The product is a stuffed felt stoplight. It sets rules in a fun way so kids will stay in bed. Each time a child gets up, he or she gets to remove one light, first the green and then the yellow. That way, the child can get out of bed for a hug or a drink of water. However, once the light is red, "It's time for bed."

Elena used the Web site Alibaba.com to find potential manufacturers in China and sent it overseas for quotes. Encouraged by how easy it was to find suppliers, she designed other parenting aids, including placemats with messages about good habits, a set of floating dice to help kids get clean in the tub, a Share Square to make sure kids take turns when playing with toys, and a time-out mat to help with discipline.

After vendors sent some initial samples, Elena developed her online presence to sell her products. The business broke even after a year, and soon after she added a line of spa products for stressed-out moms. Meanwhile, she posted hundreds of articles on free article submission sites on the web, hired an inexpensive search engine optimization expert, started a blog and electronic newsletter, and drove traffic to her site with Google, Yahoo!, and Microsoft Pay Per Click services.

Her work paid off. She won a national eBay contest that featured the business in *Entrepreneur Magazine*, was one of the top five finalists in a Yahoo! search marketing contest, and was one of five national Alibaba E-business Champions. The *Today Show* featured her products on a parenting segment, and she was profiled in a book about Alibaba. As a result of this visibility, she has been interviewed in publications around the world and appeared on local and international television shows.

Two years ago, Elena built on her former experience in four-star dining, training and placing domestic help, and teaching kids. She created the site www.etiquettemoms.com to offer programs to train trainers to teach etiquette to children and teens. The program is a major success. She now has members in thirty-nine countries and is working on expanding the etiquette programs she offers. She also launched www.artsandcraftsmoms.com to help people teach arts and crafts to kids while building their self-esteem.

Like Jaden, Elena is also generous with her advice for the stay-at-home parent:

One: Marketing has to be a priority. "You can't just put up a Web site and expect people to come and buy. You need to draw people to your site, and that's a lot of work. I'm constantly writing articles, posting blogs, keeping up with the new ways to drive traffic to a site, improving the performance of my sites, and seeking publicity for my businesses to increase my visibility."

Two: Be creative, resourceful, and tough. "I wrote an etiquette book while balancing a newborn infant on my lap. Sometimes, if the kids were acting up,

I'd have to go to my car to take a business call while my husband took care of the kids. You have to keep pushing forward, no matter how many distractions are going on around you."

Three: Let the business grow organically. "The business didn't grow exactly how I thought it would. I had no idea etiquette would be as popular as it has been. Test different ideas and build on what works."

Four: Watch for shifts in technology. "No one knows which technology will be hot in six months. We've seen blogs, social networking, different SEO strategies, Pay Per Click, Twitter, and podcasts. Stay ahead of the curve or get left behind."

Five: Be totally professional and pure. "You are always onstage. If you post something online that doesn't represent who you are or how you want to be perceived, others will see it. Stick to your message. Anything you say or do online can and, at times, will be used against you."

Six: Draw on support around you. "I rely on my husband for insights about copywriting and using the Web and for keeping the books. My mother helps me proofread my books. My kids love to test out my products. Friends critique my products and give me ideas."

Seven: This is hard work. "I think about this 24/7. If you aren't willing to work hard and push through obstacles, don't start a business."

Eight: Remember your priorities and values. "I love my business but, for me, family is first. If one of our kids is sick or having a problem at school, the business stops until we get things back on track. I know that I only get this tiny moment to watch my kids grow up. When the kids are out of the house, I can go full-time into the business."

CHAPTER 44

GOING BACK TO WORK
AFTER A LONG ABSENCE

Going back to work after a long absence can feel like you just stepped out of a time machine from the past. In addition to the earlier chapter about succeeding in your first ninety days of a new job, following are nine keys for making a successful transition back to the workforce.

One: Get up-to-speed on the latest office software. If required in your job, make sure you know how to use Microsoft Excel, PowerPoint, Word, the database program Access, Outlook, and Calendar. There are plenty of online and live training opportunities to learn these and other office programs. Learn these programs before you show up for your new job, and be sure you are learning the ones your company actually uses.

Two: Get comfortable with new ways of communicating. Learn how to use whatever smart phone is in vogue at your company, along with the right team-collaboration software, virtual meeting programs, texting, and any other mobile communication software and hardware your company might use.

Three: Stay up-to-date with technology to serve your customers. My father retired from his oncology practice for three years before going back to work part-time at a large oncology practice. He was amazed at how much technology and treatment protocols had changed in those few short years. In just about every industry, new technologies replace old ones, and you have to keep up.

Four: Follow the new rules for doing business. New laws, standards, and best practices make many of the ways we used to do things obsolete. In healthcare, the government and insurance companies constantly change how hospitals, physicians, and drug companies get paid. In banking, lending standards change. If you work in a publicly traded company, rules about disclosure, transparency, and stock options change. Keep up!

Five: Learn the new language at work. The words you use tell people whether you are on top of things or behind the times. Words change all the time. There are new management fads in the business world, new names for fancy processes, new words that resonate with current customers, and current ways of speaking that tell people you are relevant. For instance, World Wide Web used to be the way we talked about the Internet. Web log gave way to blogging. Learn the new language.

At the same time, watch out for things that used to be okay to say at the workplace and are now considered offensive and even grounds for termination. The workplace has become more politically correct than ever. Employees are sensitized to issues like sexism, racism, sexual harassment, and a hostile workplace environment. Employers will not tolerate even unintentional gaffes.

Six: Adjust to generational differences. Different generations have different values, priorities, and ways of communicating. They have different views about teamwork, how hard to work, when to give up, and loyalty to a specific company. Don't obsess about these differences or let them get in your way of achieving results, but be sensitive to them.

Seven: Don't let your ego get in the way. If you are getting back to work after an especially long absence or downshift in the economy, you may have to accept less authority, a less powerful title, and a lower salary than you used to earn. Make the best of it. Don't make a big deal to other people about how great and important you used to be. Instead, trade the old perquisites for new ones, like more flexibility, free time, and less stress.

Eight: Ask for help without seeming needy. Develop relationships with coworkers and ask them for help and advice when appropriate and while respecting their time. Ask your new boss for frequent feedback and informal reviews to make sure you are meeting his or her expectations. When you face a problem and want help, don't just dump the issue into someone else's lap. Come up with a couple of solutions and run them by the other person. That way, it is clear that you have thought through the issues and are being proactive.

Nine: Adjust responsibilities at home. If you go back to work, your family dynamics probably will change. Your spouse might need to do more childcare, grocery shopping, and cleanup. Expect some tension, and prepare for your transition back to work before you actually start. That way, everyone is supportive and on the same page.

CHAPTER 45

UNFRIENDLY FIRE AND AMBUSHES:

Saboteurs, Snipers, Jerks, Peter Principle Poster Children, Nepotism, and Difficult Bosses

I t would take thousands of pages to catalog all of the difficult types of challenging people you can encounter at work. Intentionally or unintentionally, there are people who sabotage or snipe your most important projects. There are coworkers with personality traits and communication styles that make you cringe. Some people get promoted before they are ready and make everyone else suffer. Others might be favored family members of the owner who get special treatment regardless of their talents (or lack thereof). And, of course, there are bosses who make the pointy-haired boss in Scott Adams's comic strip *Dilbert* look like a genius.

If you let these people get to you, it can derail your career and turn you into a cynic. That's because there are difficult people everywhere you go. When you quit a job without doing your best to work through issues, you might gain a reputation as someone who gives up too easily. Fortunately, you don't need a plan for each and every type of challenging person. The following six principles apply to just about any situation involving difficult people.

One: Choose to make it work. Be authentic. Stay and figure out how to deal with the other person, or leave. Don't be a hypocrite or a victim. No matter where you go, whether you work for yourself or someone else, you will always have to deal with challenging people. Make the choice to stick it out and get results.

Two: Focus on outcomes. The top way to avoid personality issues is by going back to the outcomes that everyone is working to achieve together. When everyone commits to the same outcomes, personality problems tend to become much less important, even irrelevant. At the highest levels in an organization, everyone has the same goals: increase revenues, decrease costs, dominate the competition, and create raving customers. Make sure the people around you agree on the same goals and know how those goals tie in to the organization's overall goals. When you work with people who seem to have conflicting or competing goals, find ways to help them get what they want while you get what you want, or escalate the issue to someone with the power to set priorities. With a focus on outcomes, personality problems lose their relevance. As the old business cliché advises: focus on the issue, not the person.

Three: Appreciate their strengths. Even annoying people have strengths. Focus on those and how they add value and can be useful to you. Acknowledge the other person for their contributions. Sometimes simply letting people know you appreciate them can attract them to your side.

Four: Listen and understand. It is rare that the other person is crazy. Most of the time he has a valid point of view. Take the time to understand what he is trying to achieve and what he needs. Be mature enough to make amends for things that have gone wrong in the past. Ask him for advice about how you can better work together.

Five: Set boundaries. In life as at work, you get what you tolerate. If someone's behavior is damaging productivity, morale, and results, it needs to stop. When people consistently fail to meet your explicit expectations or cross the line of acceptable behaviors, you have to set boundaries. Tell them what you expect them to do, and give them reasons to comply. You can assert appropriately without coming across as obnoxious or arrogant. If you don't take a stand, people will walk all over you.

Six: Cope. Learning to cope with and tolerate difficult people may be the best thing you can do after you exhaust the above approaches. One of my business school professors taught that around 2 percent of work is making the big and important decisions. Another 3 percent is executing on those decisions. The remaining 95 percent is coping with daily fires, difficult people, and uncertainty. As you read earlier, treat most issues at work, including challenging people, as water off a duck's back. In other words, let them go!

CHAPTER 46

DISCRIMINATION, HARASSMENT, FRAUD, PRICE-FIXING, INSIDER TRADING, KICKBACKS, AND OTHER ILLEGAL BEHAVIORS

f you encounter explicitly illegal behaviors going on in your company and you are an employee, you have three choices:

- Tolerate it and do nothing.

- Blow the whistle.

- Get out fast.

The first option is the easiest path. Simply do your job and let the illegal activities continue. You don't have to do anything different. Nobody has been caught yet, and why would they get caught now? Doesn't every company engage in some form of gray activities anyway? Why not stick with the status quo? Why not just keep your head down and assume nothing will happen? Unfortunately, things don't usually work out that way. Society has no tolerance for illegal behaviors in companies, especially these days. At some point, a scandal will break. Even if you had nothing to do with the scandal, your reputation will take a hit simply by the law of association. You or your part of the organization might even be targeted as a scapegoat, whether deserved or not. At the same time, if the company has to pay fines or loses business because of the illegal activities, your business unit might take the hit and you could lose your job. Therefore, doing nothing is not an option.

The second option, blowing the whistle, raises complications. Most forward-thinking companies have a no-tolerance policy when it comes to any kind of illegal behavior, and they have procedures in place to prevent and deal with issues. The best companies have a confidential process for employees to report any kind of illegal or even borderline ethical issues and have them dealt with. That way, you can report activities with the confidence that you will not face repercussions. Hopefully, you work for a company with strong governance that does not tolerate any kind of illegal activities. Of course, if you own the company or are in a position of power there, make sure you have these procedures and policies in place.

If you work for a company that doesn't have a confidential way for you to report issues and have them handled with integrity, then you have to decide whether you are willing to take huge personal risks in order to set things straight. Whistle-blowers are heroes, but often they take a huge hit to their careers. If you saw the movie *The Informant*, you can see how one whistle-blower, albeit extremely inept and corrupt himself, ended up getting more jail time than the people above him who were perpetuating the crimes. In warfare, guerrillas understand that surviving in the jungle comes before being a hero. You have to do what you think is right, but please consider your family and long-term career. Make sure you have an iron-clad case and a strategy to protect yourself before you blow the whistle.

The third option is most appropriate if you find yourself in a company that pushes the limits of ethical and legal behavior but you don't want to be a whistle-blower. Get out fast. There are plenty of socially responsible companies in the for-profit and nonprofit world. There are organizations out there that will fit your values and ethics. Why give yourself an ulcer wondering what will happen if you get caught up in a scandal, even if you have nothing to do with the behaviors in question? Nobody needs that kind of stress. Don't let inertia put a major red flag on your resume.

The above choices apply to explicitly illegal behaviors. Unfortunately, there are more subtle behaviors that are equally illegal but harder to document and prove. Underlying racism and sexism are examples. If you experience these situations, please visit www.bulletproofcareer.com and download the free e-book, *Success in a Challenging World*. The book was written by former NBA player Corey Crowder and me, and it features interviews with twenty-four successful African-American men and women who faced numerous setbacks. They refused to be victims or give in. Instead, they worked harder, smarter, and more effectively than their peers. They let their inner drill sergeant take over and achieved inspiring results despite their circumstances. Read their stories, and use them for guidance and courage.

CHAPTER 47

WHAT TO DO AFTER A MAJOR FAILURE

There are at least two types of failure. The first is the kind that comes with success and is systemic. A million-dollar baseball player gets called "out" seven times out of ten. A top cold-caller expects a large number of "get lost" responses before he makes a sale. The job-seeker might get rejected by many employers before getting an offer. These failures can be frustrating, but it is understood that they come with the territory. They aren't fatal as long as your average is acceptable, and with practice you can improve your winning percentage.

A second type of failure feels much more devastating. This is the really big failure that can derail your career and make you feel like someone close to you died. You get fired unexpectedly. Your business goes bankrupt. You lose your life savings after making a foolish investment. Your partner buys you out of the business and a few months later the company takes off, making him rich while you wake up screaming in the middle of the night. The economy goes south and your home is worth less than your mortgage.

When you encounter this type of failure, read the following:

- Failure merely means that a result you wanted to happen didn't. That's it. A failed result has absolutely no bearing on your worth as a person. Your idea or plans might have failed, but YOU are not a failure. You still have your talents, brains, and energy. Chalk the result up to a great life experience and learn whatever lessons you can. At the very least, learn enough so you don't make the same mistakes again. Get back out there and never look back.

- If you failed while trying to grow a business, realize that you had the courage to do something many people never have the guts to even dream about, much less try. Our entire economic system depends on entrepreneurs like you. Our government cannot function without risk-takers like you, nor can the many people who cannot or will not provide for themselves. You are a hero, even if you didn't achieve your goal.

- Don't let anyone else define you. If other people judge you because you tried to achieve something and didn't quite make it, they are usually projecting their own fears and insecurities onto you. If others label you as a failure, ignore them. Shed them from your life. Surround yourself with positive people who understand that life is full of risk. Only people who are truly alive take risks and try to make great things happen.

- Ultimate failure comes only when you fall down and refuse to get up again. Fighters know this. When they get knocked down, they get up and do their best to come back the next round. When they get knocked out, they get up, congratulate the opponent, and train harder than ever to win the next fight. Get back up and keep punching!

- Give thanks for what you have, and use the experience to get closer to the people and things in your life that really matter. In my own case, when my wife and I lost a huge amount of money on my foolish foray into the professional mixed-martial-arts fighting business, we had a moment I'll never forget. I was really scared about the impact the business might have on my family, and I asked her if she would still love me even if we lost our home and had to live in a trailer. She hugged me and said, "Of course." Then she was silent for a minute and added, "But let's shut down this business before that happens, okay?" At that moment, I realized more than ever before how important my family was to me. I've felt more grounded about my true priorities ever since.

- Take comfort in the many, many people who have failed big, sometimes many times, only to become huge successes later on. Michael Jordan was cut from his high school basketball team. Walt Disney's first production went bankrupt. Winston Churchill failed the sixth grade. Steven Spielberg was put in learning-disabled class in junior high. Before achieving icon status, Marilyn Monroe was dropped by 20th Century Fox one year into her contract with them; they thought she was unattractive and couldn't act. John Grisham faced rejection from a dozen publishing houses and almost the same number of agents when he tried to publish his first novel. Abraham Lincoln completed only about five years of formal education, failed in two business ventures, and lost eight elections before becoming one of the

United States' great presidents. Warren Buffet was crushed when Harvard Business School rejected his application for admission to their program. The Beatles were quickly rejected during their first audition with a label. Elvis Presley was fired by the manager of the Grand Ole Opry after one night and told he would never amount to anything. Chester Carlson faced seven years of rejection before he sold the rights to his copy machine invention to the company now known as Xerox. Lucille Ball was kicked out of drama school and told she was too shy to be successful as an actor.

Still not convinced? Do a search of "famous high school dropouts" on Google for a list of highly successful people who never graduated from college or even high school. There are thousands, in all walks of life, including Bill Gates and his fellow Microsoft founder Paul Allen, photographer Ansel Adams, author Jane Austen, entrepreneur Richard Branson, philanthropist Andrew Carnegie, Michael Dell, Oracle founder Larry Ellison, Napster founder Shawn Fanning, real estate developer Thomas Flatley, and many, many, many more. Keep researching famous failures until you get the point: failure can be a milestone on the way to success, assuming you learn from your mistakes and keep moving forward in more effective ways.

CONCLUSION:
Your Next Steps

One of the harder things I ever did was climbing to the top of the ropes course and tower at the Sarasota YMCA. I was out of shape and not a natural climber. About halfway up, I got stuck. I was breathing hard and felt like I should just let go and let my harness take me back to the ground.

Meanwhile, the instructor kept yelling: "One more step! Just take one more step!"

I got my breath back and took just one more step. Then I rested while the instructor yelled, "Just take one more step." I took one more step.

A few minutes later, I reached the top.

That patient instructor's advice continues to echo in my mind whenever I hit hard times. Rather than give up, I find a way to take one more step. I don't plan out every single next step in excruciating detail, because that will overwhelm me. I don't calculate how much farther I have to go, because that will depress me. I just take one more step.

It is popular today to use magical thinking and New Age approaches to get ahead, as if simply visualizing a goal is enough to make it happen. That's not the guerrilla way. Success requires passion, resilience, relationships, and practical action. You have to keep taking that next step, no matter how frustrated and tired you feel.

What's your next step to advance your career and be ready for anything that comes at you?

- What is one step you can take to strengthen an important relationship in your power base?

- What is one step you can take to meet someone who can bring value to your career?

- What is one step you can take to further build your expertise in your chosen field?

- What is one step you can take to come closer to achieving your most ambitious and inspiring dream for your career?

- What is one step you can take to strengthen your personal financial picture?

- What is one step you can take to anticipate and avoid a risk or potential ambush that could derail your career?

- What is one step you can take to begin developing a flip-the-switch backup plan?

As you consider your next step, here is one must-do: visit www.bulletproofcareer.com. That way we can continue the journey you started with this book. The site gives you many additional free resources to take that next step and keep moving your career forward while staying bulletproof.

Jay and I wish you great success!

ABOUT THE AUTHORS

Jay Conrad Levinson is the author of the best-selling marketing series in history, *Guerrilla Marketing*, plus fifty-eight other business books. His books have sold more than 21 million copies worldwide. His guerrilla concepts have influenced marketing so much that his books appear in sixty-two languages and are required reading in MBA programs worldwide.

He was born in Detroit, raised in Chicago, and graduated from the University of Colorado. His studies in psychology led him to advertising agencies, including a directorship at Leo Burnett in London, where he served as Creative Director. Returning to the United States, he joined J. Walter Thompson as senior VP. Jay created and taught guerrilla marketing for ten years at the extension division of the University of California in Berkeley.

A winner of first prizes in all forms of media, he has been part of the creative teams that made household names of the Marlboro Man, the Pillsbury Doughboy, Allstate's Good Hands, United Airlines' Friendly Skies, the Sears Diehard battery, Morris the Cat, Mr. Clean, Tony the Tiger, and the Jolly Green Giant.

Today, *Guerrilla Marketing* is the most powerful brand in the history of marketing, listed among the 100 best business books ever written, with a popular Web site at www.gmarketing.com. The brand also powers The Guerrilla Marketing Association—a support system for small business.

Although Jay is able to list those notable accomplishments, he believes the *most* notable is that, since 1971, he has worked a three-day week from his home.

After living in the San Francisco Bay Area for thirty-five years, Jay and Jeannie Levinson sold their home, bought an RV, towed a Jeep, and ended up, six years later, at their lakefront home outside Orlando, Florida, and close to their twenty-six grandchildren, their own personal Disney World. Nobody on earth is as qualified to tell you about guerrilla marketing as the Father of Guerrilla Marketing, Jay Conrad Levinson.

Andrew Neitlich is the founder and director of the Center for Executive Coaching at www. centerforexecutivecoaching.com, along with sister organizations The Center for Career Coaching at www. centerforcareercoaching.com and The Institute for Business Growth at www.instituteforbusinessgrowth. com. These organizations train coaches and aspiring coaches from around the world to work with executives and business owners. Andrew received his undergraduate degree from Harvard College in 1987 and his MBA from Harvard Business School in 1991. Andrew's career has included stints as an employee, consultant, coach, executive, business owner, investor, and interim executive. His industry experience includes consumer goods, healthcare, technology, nonprofit, finance, publishing, education, and professional sports. He lives with his wife Elena and three children Noah, Seth, and Willow in Sarasota, Florida, where he plays tennis almost every day.

CLAIM YOUR FREE BONUS WORTH $497!

Go to www.bulletproofcareer.com right now and enter the password GMCAREER. You immediately get exclusive access to:

- Additional **FREE** career success strategies, resources, tools, and how-to guides;

- **FREE** step-by-step details about launching the flip-the-switch backup plans described in the book;

- Invitations to **FREE** live teleconferences with the author about career and business success;

- **FREE** podcasts and mp3 recordings about career success strategies;

- A **FREE** resource directory that lists the key websites you need to know to propel your career forward;

- The **FREE** ebook *Success in a Challenging World*, featuring interviews with 24 inspiring people who overcame significant obstacles to succeed in their career and in life; and

- A **FREE** set of financial calculators to pay down debt, plan your savings, and get your financial house in order so you have a buffer in case you get ambushed.

No additional purchase is required. Don't miss out on the opportunity to propel your career further and keep up to date with the top trends in career success.

Go to www.bulletproofcareer.com and register now.
The password is GMCAREER.

REMEMBER – If you got value from this book, tell a friend or colleague about it. People will appreciate you for letting them know about a resource that can help them.

To learn more about
Guerrilla Marketing
and Jay Conrad Levinson,
visit <u>www.gmarketing.com</u>.

BUY A SHARE OF THE FUTURE IN YOUR COMMUNITY

These certificates make great holiday, graduation and birthday gifts that can be personalized with the recipient's name. The cost of one S.H.A.R.E. or one square foot is $54.17. The personalized certificate is suitable for framing and will state the number of shares purchased and the amount of each share, as well as the recipient's name. The home that you participate in "building" will last for many years and will continue to grow in value.

Here is a sample SHARE certificate:

THIS CERTIFIES THAT

YOUR NAME HERE

HAS INVESTED IN A HOME FOR A DESERVING FAMILY

1985-2005

TWENTY YEARS OF BUILDING FUTURES IN OUR COMMUNITY ONE HOME AT A TIME

1200 SQUARE FOOT HOUSE @ $65,000 = $54.17 PER SQUARE FOOT
This certificate represents a tax deductible donation. It has no cash value.

YES, I WOULD LIKE TO HELP!

I support the work that Habitat for Humanity does and I want to be part of the excitement! As a donor, I will receive periodic updates on your construction activities but, more importantly, I know my gift will help a family in our community realize the dream of homeownership. **I would like to SHARE in your efforts against substandard housing in my community!** *(Please print below)*

PLEASE SEND ME _____ SHARES at $54.17 EACH = $ $_____

In Honor Of: _____

Occasion: (Circle One)   HOLIDAY   BIRTHDAY   ANNIVERSARY

  OTHER: _____

Address of Recipient: _____

Gift From: _____ *Donor Address:* _____

Donor Email: _____

I AM ENCLOSING A CHECK FOR $ $_____ PAYABLE TO HABITAT FOR HUMANITY OR PLEASE CHARGE MY VISA OR MASTERCARD *(CIRCLE ONE)*

Card Number _____ Expiration Date: _____

Name as it appears on Credit Card _____ Charge Amount $ _____

Signature _____

Billing Address _____

Telephone # Day _____ Eve _____

PLEASE NOTE: Your contribution is tax-deductible to the fullest extent allowed by law.
Habitat for Humanity • P.O. Box 1443 • Newport News, VA 23601 • 757-596-5553
www.HelpHabitatforHumanity.org

LaVergne, TN USA
04 February 2011
215236LV00003B/2/P